Applying Advanced
Analytics to
HR Management
Decisions

Applying Advanced Analytics to HR Management Decisions

Methods for Selection, Developing Incentives, and Improving Collaboration

James C. Sesil

Vice President, Publisher: Tim Moore
Associate Publisher and Director of Marketing: Amy Neidlinger
Executive Editor: Jeanne Glasser Levine
Operations Specialist: Jodi Kemper
Cover Designer: Alan Clements
Managing Editor: Kristy Hart
Project Editor: Elaine Wiley
Copy Editor: Keith Cline
Proofreader: Sarah Kearns
Indexer: Tim Wright
Compositor: Nonie Ratcliff
Manufacturing Buyer: Dan Uhrig

© 2014 by Pearson Education, Inc.

Publishing as Pearson

Upper Saddle River, New Jersey 07458

Pearson offers excellent discounts on this book when ordered in quantity for bulk purchases or special sales. For more information, please contact U.S. Corporate and Government Sales, 1-800-382-3419, corpsales@pearsontechgroup.com. For sales outside the U.S., please contact International Sales at international@pearsoned.com.

Company and product names mentioned herein are the trademarks or registered trademarks of their respective owners.

Printed in the United States of America

First Printing October 2013

ISBN-10: 0-13-306460-3
ISBN-13: 978 0-13-306460-5

Pearson Education LTD.
Pearson Education Australia PTY, Limited.
Pearson Education Singapore, Pte. Ltd.
Pearson Education Asia, Ltd.
Pearson Education Canada, Ltd.
Pearson Educación de Mexico, S.A. de C.V.
Pearson Education—Japan
Pearson Education Malaysia, Pte. Ltd.

Library of Congress Control Number: 2013943653

To Kathy and Al

Contents

Acknowledgments

I need to thank many for helping this book become tangible. My interest in this topic extends back to my graduate school days at the University of Minnesota and internships at the Control Data Corporation and Honeywell, Inc. It was further developed working for Cargill, Inc., in the United States, and for Cargill, Plc. as an expatriate in London. Some of the groundwork was done while working on my Ph.D. at the London School of Economics and working at the Centre for Economic Performance at the LSE. It was further developed while teaching at Rutgers and during my summers at the Athens Laboratory of Business Administration in Greece. The actual writing got underway during my time as a Fulbright Scholar at the City University of Hong Kong.

Specifically, I want to thank the following friends and associates: Debra Norman, Doug Kruse, Steve Director, Richard Freeman, Barbara Lee, Charles Fay, Joseph Blasi, Mark Huselid, Randall Schuler, Susan Jackson, Corey Rosen, Olga Epitropaki, Vinney Senguttuvan, Sameer Maskey, Odette–Simone Smolicz, Kwok Leung, Brian Dominick, Kathleen Turco-Lyon, Charlotte Matthews, Laurie Rudman, Bob Jorissen, Rick Synder, Al Bleich, Terry Park, Maya Kroumova, Yu Peng Lin, Rena Morrissey, Amanda Salter, Lorraine Wrafter, James Kohrt, Bob Ernt, Peter Price, Darryl Sjoberg, Ansgar Richter, Steve Machin, Martin Conyon, Alan Manning, David Metcalf, Jonathon Wadsworth, Danny Quah, Richard Layard, Paul Gregg, Shulun Chang-Reuter, Ching-Bin Lin, Ethan Tsai, Arthur Langer, David Murphy, Jack McGourty.

Many of my former students were instrumental in helping me to develop my thinking on these matters.

I would also like to thank Martin Rugfelt and others at Expert Maker for access to their excellent software.

My sincere thanks to Paula Caligiuri and Jeanne Glasser for their support.

My sister, Christine Schultz; and brothers, Joseph Sesil, Daniel Sesil; brother-in-law, Steve Schultz; sister-in-law Teresa Sesil; my lovely nieces and nephew; and my wonderful extended family, the Payants.

I would especially like to thank my friend Antonia Marquardt for our many careful and thoughtful conversations on topics covered in this book.

Funding from the Consulate General of the United States Hong Kong and Macau and the organizing body for the Fulbright Scholars Program, the Council for International Exchange of Scholars (CIES) is gratefully acknowledged.

Any and all errors are, of course, my own.

About the Author

James C. Sesil is currently developing state-of-the-art HR decision support software utilizing the newest machine learning and AI technologies. He has ten years' experience teaching at the London School of Economics, Rutgers University, and City University of Hong Kong.

Sesil's work has won three best paper awards from the Academy of Management and the Labor and Employment Research Association and has been covered in *The New York Times*, *BusinessWeek*, and *The Financial Times*. He spent eight years in HR roles at Control Data, Honeywell, and Cargill, Inc., and he holds a Ph.D. from the London School of Economics.

Preface

Written for anyone in any organization making human capital management (HCM) decisions, including C-level executives and all managers, this book does several things:

- It provides a summary of implications associated with new research on how decisions are made and what motivates us.

- It develops an evidence-based approach using advanced analytics to assist organizations with developing a collaborative workplace and with selecting and motivating people.

- It applies the new thinking associated with advances in behavioral economics, psychology, and machine learning to the decision-making process and refers to this as "The New Human Science."

- And it further recognizes the value of human experience and expertise and provides a mechanism for applying both advanced analytics and intuition or expert knowledge.

Here is how the book is structured.

Chapter 1, "Challenges and Opportunities with Optimal Decision Making and How Advanced Analytics Can Help," provides the overall framework and discusses how it is to be applied to human capital management (HCM) decision making. This framework builds on the work of Nobel Prize winning social psychologist Daniel Kahneman, along with others, to provide strong evidence that we do not decide rationally. The chapter discusses the role biases play in decision making and how the use of advanced analytics can help eliminate bias from decisions.

Chapter 2, "Collaboration, Cooperation, and Reciprocity," focuses on the role of collaboration, information sharing, and decentralized decision making. In this chapter, some of the old thinking about what motivates us is dispelled, and new findings are applied. Economic science has long held that we are generally self-centered, selfish, inherently lazy, and largely interested in only income maximization. This assumption about our natures has had a substantial impact on the way in which the employment relationship has been structured and has generally led to mistrust and noncooperative behaviors. Recent evidence finds that we are actually unselfish, cooperative, altruistic, and potentially very self-motivated. This has substantial implications for how we ideally organize ourselves. The role and importance of collaboration and cooperation is also discussed.

Chapter 3, "Value Creation and Advanced Analytics," covers evidence where value is found within organizations and how getting the right mix of human capital, HCM practices and policies, and technology will ultimately lead to better performance outcomes. The loss associated with high employee turnover is discussed, as is how human science can help reduce the loss of expertise associated with human capital leaving the organization.

Chapter 4, "Human Science and Selection Decisions," covers how advanced analytics can reduce and eliminate discriminatory hiring and promotion decisions. The focus of the chapter is on the use of bio data to make better hiring predictions.

Chapter 5, "Human Science and Incentives," focuses on how advanced analytics can assist with decisions associated with developing incentive contracts. New evidence on what motivates people is discussed, as well as how a focus on tournament compensation is suboptimal. Application of human science including advanced analytics to practical incentive contract challenges is made.

Introduction

The New Human Science and HCM Decisions

I am a runner. I have completed 23 marathons and more half-marathons, 10k, and 5k races than I can remember. So in 2010 when I went in for my annual physical and was told that I had the loudest heart murmur the examining physician had ever encountered, I thought she had a seriously faulty stethoscope. Nonetheless, I took her advice and went in for an EKG and discovered I did indeed have a seriously faulty heart. I had mitral value prolapse with flail (MVPWF)—essentially, one of my values was not closing and I needed surgery to have it repaired or replaced. So, being a research-oriented type of person who really wanted to keep running, I learned everything I could about MVPWF and starting looking around for a great cardiovascular surgeon. I sent the video of my faulty heart value to surgeons around the country and discussed my options with a number of them. I examined and evaluated all the data I could find on my condition and what could be done about it. I also did a lot of due diligence when choosing a surgeon. The one I finally chose had all the right numbers, but what sealed the deal for me was his office walls were covered with pictures of all the hearts he had fixed. When I saw the way his face lit up when he started to talk about his wall of hearts, I knew I had the right guy, and I did.

My choice of a surgeon was a selection decision, plain and simple. Though I did not realize it at the time, it was also a case study in data and intuitive decision making. I am a fact guy; it is really important to me to make as optimal a decision as possible, but I also have learned to trust my instincts. The data analyzed and research I did was critical for making an optimal decision, but just as important was my own intuition. There is still no software application, supercomputer, or A.I. tool that can touch our ability to assess certain intangibles.

The use of analytics has a long history associated with human capital management (HCM) decisions, but far too many organizations continue to use these tools for reporting simple descriptive statistics and correlations. Advanced analytics has been adopted by other business functions such as finance and marketing; however, it still has a long way to go to be fully utilized for HCM decisions. According to research conducted by IBM in which 700 chief human resource officers were interviewed, less than 25% are using sophisticated analytics to predict future outcomes and for decision making.[1]

The underutilization of advanced analytics associated with HCM decisions is a problem because the jury is in: There is a real and direct bottom-line impact associated with getting these decisions right. If an organization wants to deliver the highest quality goods and services, superior customer service, and the most innovative products, effective HCM is required. Getting HCM right boils down to making many decisions and making them correctly.

The challenge and opportunity is that the entire range of HCM decisions (from where and how to recruit and hire, how to reward and motivate, and which policy and practice to use in a specific situation) is getting very difficult to make optimally. There are a huge number of different practices and policies and combinations to choose from and an ever-increasing amount of pertinent information useful for making these decisions. Fortunately, there is new research, insights, analytical tools, and processes associated with advanced analytics that can assist in making these decisions much more optimally. For example, companies like Xerox and Google are using predictive analytics to evaluate which characteristics are associated with good employees, and this information is used to help with employee selection.[2] The use of advanced analytics can help eliminate all forms of bias associated with selection and promotion decisions and also provide a mechanism for compensating and rewarding people in a more accurate and fair manner.

If biases are eliminated from the decision-making process, previously unconsidered possibilities will emerge. SAP, the German software giant, has announced that by the year 2020, 1% of its workforce will fall on the autistic spectrum. The company has found greater engagement and productivity in locations where they have adopted this hiring policy.[3] Some of the most productive and capable computer programmers fall on the autistic spectrum. By undermining any prejudice and bias associated with autism, SAP is potentially developing a previously unrecognized HCM competitive advantage. Advanced analytics can aid in the process of identifying these possibilities by eliminating all extraneous factors from decision making so that only merit and potential is taken into consideration.

A number of factors are converging that make this the right time to start using data and other information to make more robust decisions. Technology has become more accessible, user friendly, and powerful. There have been recent advances in machine learning, natural language, and deep Q&A expert systems (for example, IBM's Watson beating two former *Jeopardy!* champions). In addition, we know substantially more about what really contributes to organizational performance (for instance, balance scorecards and intangible capital), and we are also getting much better at modeling what is important to people and how people think and how they actually behave (for example, behavioral psychology, behavioral economics, and neuroeconomics).

Many of these paradigm-shifting developments have *not* been incorporated into our decision-making processes. It has long been held that we humans are rational decision makers who are very self-centered and selfish. Recent research has shown that we are rarely inclined to make rational decisions and that we are actually very cooperative, collaborative, and unselfish and want to be treated fairly and to see others treated the same.[4] These finding have tremendous implications for how we manage the employment relationship. Equity matters because it matters to the primary input in all organizations' output equation: human capital.[5] Humans want to be treated and rewarded fairly. If they are not, they withhold value-creating information and effort, are more likely to be absent, quit, and sometime actively conspire to undermine the goals of the organization.

I refer to all these recent findings as "The New Human Science." I integrate the recent findings on what motivates us, what influences our decision making, and what our natures are like, with recent advances in technology in order to assist us with making more optimal value-creating decisions.

This is not to suggest that advanced analytics will replace human expertise. Instead, I believe that it will complement it. In 1997, the chess master Gary Kasparov lost to the IBM computer Deep Blue. However, as Kasparov later reported, the most unbeatable champion is not a supercomputer. The most powerful computer can be beat by a good amateur chess player working with a standard PC. The optimal decision maker is not computer or human alone, but rather the combination.[6] That is the position taken in this book. When well-seasoned human expertise is combined with the right advanced analytics, the decisions made will be much more likely to create value for everyone.

There is data and there is data. I will be talking about techniques, but equally important is to get the questions right. The tools have gotten really cool and the types of analysis that are now possible were not even imagined ten years ago. None of that changes the fact that data is really about stories. In the case of this book, stories are about what is going on in your organization—what (and whom) is working and what is not. Everything that is discussed here is meant to help us become better and more accurate data story tellers.

Some might view big data, advanced analytics, and data science as being sterile and potentially dehumanizing. I argue the exact opposite. The use of these tools, when coupled with the right kind of human expertise, can help us become much more *humane* decision makers. By humane, I mean fairer, inclusive, and merit based—ultimately making our organizations more equitable, collaborative, and successful.

One final note. This book is meant to be used in conjunction with its associated website, DecisionAnalyticsInc.com. The focus of the book is on what can and should be done with advanced analytics and optimal HCM decision making. The website will provide tools and more detail on exactly *how* this this optimal decision making is accomplished.

1

Challenges and Opportunities with Optimal Decision Making and How Advanced Analytics Can Help

1.1 How We Make Decisions and What Gets in the Way

In their book *Nudge,* economist Richard Thayler and legal scholar Cass Sunstein describe homo economicus and homo sapiens. Homo economicus are humans as they are described in economics text-books. They act and make decisions completely rationally, have the computing power of a hundred super computers, and they always know precisely what will make them happy. Homo sapiens, however, do things like jump out of perfectly good airplanes, forget significant others' birthdays, and occasionally drink or eat too much. Thaler and Sunstein refer to homo economicus as econs and refer to the rest of us as humans.[1]

Remarkably, until relatively recently, even in light of nearly unlimited anecdotal and empirical evidence, we *assumed* our decision making was almost always rational and optimal. It was not until the ground-breaking work of those like Thayler, Daniel Kahneman, Amos Tversky, Robyn Dawes, Daniel Ariely, and many others that this fundamental assumption of rationality was largely undone. Probably the fatal blow to the idea that we always decide rationally was delivered by

Kahnman and Tversky.[2] "Econs" have long been assumed to "maximize their utility"; this requires that they have a very clear idea of preferences. Work by Tversky and Kahneman provide evidence of a "framing effect."[3] This finding shows that our preferences and subsequent decisions will be impacted depending on how the information is presented.

Relative to human capital management (HCM) decisions, this may mean that someone is rejected for an interview based on the letter font used on his curriculum vitae (CV) or resumé. It might not be a conscious decision; the reviewer may just equate a particular style with professionalism. Though most would agree presentation matters, making a decision to not interview someone based on one data point, and that data point being a preference for Times New Roman over Cambria, could be considered less than ideal. This matters because the sum total of all the small and large HCM decisions *will* make or break an organization. Who we hire and promote, how we compensate and motivate people, the type of training they receive—these decisions have a direct and identifiable impact on the success of the organization.[4]

Though there is an ongoing debate about just how rational we really are,[5] there is agreement that we are often pushed toward acting irrationally,[6] even when rational action would lead to the best outcomes. I conduct empirical research, and the research questions that interest me evolve around this question: What works at work? For example, does giving employees more decision-making authority lead to better firm performance? Does the executive compensation plan provide an incentive to actually improve performance?

One topic on which I have done a fair amount of research is the granting of stock options to nonexecutive employees.[7] From the perspective of standard rational economic theory, this is really a foolish thing to do. Economic theory would say that granting stock options to anyone other than the top few employees is about as sensible as burning the options. The primary theoretical lens used to justify granting company shares to employees is called *agency theory,* and although it provides a very good rationale for the granting of stock options to executives, it provides a very poor one for granting to non-executives.[8] Based on agency theory, there is no reason to expect giving stock options to nonexecutive employees will motivate them to work harder, smarter, or longer, because their individual efforts have very little impact on the share price. However, surprisingly, initially even to me, giving stock options to nonexecutive employees seems to do just that. We have repeatedly found evidence that giving stock options to a broad set of employees (in some cases, everyone in the firm) increases productivity and other performance outcomes.[9] So, this would argue that in this instance, employees are not acting as one would expect econs to act. Instead of making people work harder because they think their work can move the share price, they appear to be working harder because of some completely different reason.

A detailed exploration of what is driving those behaviors is beyond our scope here, but it may be that broad-based stock options create a culture of engagement. Stock options may go some way toward establishing a workplace where there is an attitude that we are all in this together, and maybe this is what causes employees to work harder, smarter, longer, or more collaboratively.[10] What this means is that when we are attempting to predict how people are *actually* going to respond, the rationale model is not of much use. (Like it or not, our default assumption is often that people will respond rationally.) It also means that our *predictive models* need to incorporate new findings from behavioral economics, psychology, and neuroeconomics.

In an interview conducted in the *Sloan Management Review,* Thomas Davenport, who, along with Jeanne Harris, has written extensively on analytics, said that he thought many great tools were being underutilized.[11] In the article, Davenport went on to say that not only was he referring to structured and unstructured data but also to the insights on decision making that could be found in the "wisdom of crowds," "behavioral economics," and "neuroscience." This section explores a number of the factors that impact the quality of our decision making.

1.1.1 Intuition Versus Analytical Thinking

The fact that we do not decide rationally is not to suggest that there is anything wrong with the way our brains work; after all, it is our minds that came up with things like language, the written word, chocolate-covered peanuts (significant and important things). Daniel Kahneman's, notion of thinking fast and slow and Thayler and Sunstein's System 1 and System 2 cover the important characteristics of how we think. Thinking fast is essentially making decisions based on intuition, and thinking slow, as the name implies, refers to making decisions based primarily on analytical evaluation. Kahneman also uses the terms *System 1* and *System 2* thinking. System 1 thinking is our intuition—those thoughts, feelings, impressions, associations, and preparations for action that all happen automatically and fast (for example, chatting with friends or brushing our teeth). System 2 thinking, reflective thinking, is by contrast slow and deliberate, thoughtful and effortful. This is the type of thinking we engage in when rule-based logic is required or when, for example, we are completing our taxes or learning a new skill. Examples of situations where we think fast include the following:[12]

- Detect that one object is more distant than another

- Detect hostility in a voice

- Understand simple sentences

At other times, our thinking needs to slow considerably, as in the following examples:[13]

- Teaching someone a new skill

- Filling out a survey

- Checking the validity of a complex logical argument

Basing decisions solely on intuition can be problematic. Making hiring, promotion, and bonus decisions based on gut instinct carries with it the potential for including a lot of bias and incomplete information. The fact is that most workforce management decisions are rife with potential biases, and making these decisions with the assistance of analytics can help eliminate many of these biases. This is not to say that there is no place for "expert" intuitive knowledge. The use of stock options is an example. Based purely on a rational model of decision making, no firm would ever issue stock options to anyone other than the two or three top employees who may have the power to move the share price.

Silicon Valley, the undisputed epicenter of worldwide technological innovation, was one of the first to recognize how broadly distributed stock options could help motivate and retain employees.[14] In fact, some say that stock options provide the fuel that powers Silicon Valley.[15] Frankly, Silicon Valley might never have existed (and so some of the world's greatest innovations might not have happened) if those making HCM decisions had thought like econs and assumed everyone else did too.

What you want to keep in mind here is that although there is a critical role for intuition (that is, paying attention to your gut), it is almost always advisable to temper decisions with analytics. Generally speaking, many of the decisions associated with HCM have considerable potential for bias. Consequently, the ideal approach is one that combines the best analytics with well-seasoned human expertise.

1.1.2 Poor Intuitive Statisticians

Another critical realization is that we are really lousy statisticians. In the introduction to his book, Kahneman recounts the story of the first research project that he and Tversky undertook. They wanted to determine how good we are as intuitive statisticians. So, they developed and administered a survey at a meeting for the Society of Mathematical Psychology; participants included those who had authored statistical textbooks.[16] Even those with years of training and expertise were not good at predicting the probability of an event. Those with substantial training in statistics were prone to accept research that was based on small sample sizes and also gave a hypothetical graduate student inaccurate advice regarding the number of observations she would have to collect. This matters because we are constantly accessing the probability of an event occurring (for example, the probability that an employee will perform as expected, the likelihood that a specific compensation approach will promote desirable outcomes). Fortunately, there is a fix, or at least a fairly robust solution. Data coupled with a good idea of the factors influencing an outcome, along with some pretty straightforward statistics, will go a long way toward predicting a likely outcome.

1.1.3 Understanding Human Nature

In a book about advanced analytics, it might strike you as odd that I will also be emphasizing the critical role that human intuition plays in decision making. I emphasize this because a number of constraints apply to advanced analytics when attempting to *predict* how people are actually going to act. Take, for example, stock options. Any model that expects rational behavior would expect no incentive effect associated with their use. (For example, individuals should not work longer, harder, or smarter.) However, that is not what we observe. People do actually work much harder. The more we understand how people think and act and what is important and what motives them, the greater the likelihood that we can accurately *predict* behaviors. Much new evidence from the natural and social sciences helps us better understand human nature; the same holds true for the humanities. For instance, experimental philosophy is empirically testing many basic assumptions about how we experience and relate to the world.[17] We delve into the implications of these new findings in subsequent chapters.

1.1.4 Biases and Decisions

One of the most critical factors influencing our decision making is our own biases. These are not something that we are generally even consciously aware of. However, they adversely impact our decisions making. A number of biases are especially troublesome when making HCM decisions, including the following:[18]

- **Confirmation bias:** This bias causes us to ignore evidence that undermines a preconceived idea. For instance, we may be convinced that someone is the person for the job even after much evidence to the contrary.

- **Anchoring:** We have a tendency to focus on data points that we consider to be especially telling. For instance, when making hiring decisions, college grade point average may weigh heavily, even though it has not been shown to be a good predictor of job performance.

  Anchoring refers to our tendency to weigh this one data point too greatly when making decisions.

- **Loss aversion:** This bias refers to our tendency to weigh potential losses greater than potential gains. We come by this bias honestly; there is an evolutionary advantage to focus on potential threats (hungry predators) rather than focusing on long term planning.

- **Status quo:** This bias is the tendency to go along with the status quo or the default option.[19]

- **Framing:** You can find an excellent example of framing in an article by Paul J. H. Schoemaker and J. Edward Russo.[20] Managers were asked what how they would respond to the following situation:

"Assume you are the vice president of manufacturing in a Fortune 500 company that employs over 130,000 people with annual sales exceeding $10 billion. Due to the recession as well as structural changes in your industry, one of your factories (with 600 employees) is faced with either a complete or partial shutdown. You and your staff carefully narrowed the options to either:

A. Scale back and keep a few production lines open. Exactly 400 jobs will be lost (out of 600).

B. Invest in new equipment that may or may not improve your competitive position. There is a 1/3 chance that no jobs will be lost but a 2/3 chance all 600 jobs will be lost.

Financially, these options are equally attractive (in expected rate of return). The major difference is the effect of the decision on the plant workers, who have stood by the company for many hard years without unionizing. Which option would you choose if these were your only alternatives?"

The exercise is repeated and this time the options are slightly reworded.

A. "Scale back and keep a few production lines open. Exactly 200 jobs will be saved (out of 600 threatened by layoff).

B. Invest in new equipment that may or may not improve your competitive position. There is a 1/3 chance all jobs will be saved but a 2/3 chance that none of the 600 jobs will be saved."[21]

Tellingly, when "framed" in the first example, most managers choose option A. When framed by the second, most managers choose the opposite.

These and other biases that are discussed in later chapters all serve to undermine the quality of many decisions generally and HCM decisions specifically.

1.1.5 Big Data and Information Overload

We are in the age of very, very big data. Just how big? Pretty big. Table 1.1 describes various quantities of bytes.[22]

Table 1.1 Byte Measurements

Name	Value
Kilobyte (KB)	10^3
Megabyte (MB)	10^6
Gigabyte (GB)	10^9
Terabyte (TB)	10^{12}
Petabyte (PB)	10^{15}
Exabyte (EB)	10^{18}
Zettabyte (ZB)	10^{21}
Yottabyte (YB)	10^{24}

The amount of data in "big data" is simply staggering. There are roughly one billion transistors per person and four billion cell phone users.[23] According to Gartner, the amount of information is growing at 59% annually,[24] and much of this information is unstructured data in the form of video, social media, blogs, and so on. There is simply too much information for our brains to process adequately. The brain itself can be thought of as a tremendous data producing mechanism, given that it contains 85 to 100 billion neurons and produces roughly 300,000 petabytes of data each year.[25] For some time now, we have had more information than we can process, and the ongoing exponential increase in information (information explosion) exacerbates this situation. One place where computers have us beat is in processing tremendous amounts of information very, very fast.

1.1.6 The Problem with Certitude

During dinner once with a former colleague and her husband, *Raiders of the Lost Ark* came up as we were talking about movies. We started discussing the scene in which Marian (played by Karen Allen) won a drinking game in the bar she owned. My former colleague was absolutely certain that the person she drank under the table was Indiana Jones (Harrison Ford). *Raiders of the Lost Ark* was one of my favorite movies, so I knew differently. I told her that it was actually some otherwise unknown local, not Indy. So certain that she was right, she said that she would bet her house it was Jones. The words of some wise sage popped into my head: "If someone offers you a perfectly good house, take it." So, I took the bet, and we headed down to the local video rental store. However, I was starting to have mixed feelings about actually taking their house, so I told them that I would be happy to let them off the hook and drop the bet. This elicited some pretty dodgy accusations about my stomach for betting. So, as long as they insisted.... Before watching the movie, I asked my former colleague (who is extremely bright and one of the top academics in her field) what she considered to be the probability of her being correct. She said 99.9999%. In other words, she was sure that she was right, really sure. Anyone who has seen the movie and remembers that scene will know that I won a house. In case you are interested, I let them stay in their home, but I was not above occasionally asking whether they were taking good care of my property. I am not sharing this story to spotlight my movie knowledge. Instead, I want to point out that just because we really, really think we are right does not mean that we necessarily are. And trust me, I have been guilty of this more than once.

1.1.7 Advanced Analytics Does Not Care Who It Annoys

Unfortunately, some in positions of authority have fragile egos or are primarily concerned with advancing their own agenda rather than dealing with actual facts. Hiring yes men and yes women is simply a losing proposition. Warren Buffett, for instance, goes out of his way to seek out people to tell him that he is wrong, and many (if not all) successful organizations never become self-satisfied. One of the big advantages of advanced analytics is that it is entirely immune to big egos, group think, and the loudest getting their way.

Evolution has favored those who are good at advancing an argument, whether or not the argument is based on fact, and so we come by our opinionated natures honestly. The challenge arises when the focus shifts from getting to the truth of the matter to winning the argument instead. Of course, we hope, those who are right win. Unfortunately, though, the evidence indicates that this is not always the case. The April 2011 issue of the *Journal of Behavioral and Brain Sciences* was devoted to the theory of argumentative reasoning.[26] The theory holds that we developed rationality not as a result of our desire to pursue philosophical and scientific insight and to develop a superior morality, but rather we developed it to win arguments. When it comes to winning arguments, what matters is certitude—knowing, or at least projecting, that you are certain you are right. Those skilled at winning arguments are advancing arguments rather than looking for the truth. All too often, therefore, "cherry picking" of the facts takes place. Here is where more sophisticated analytical models can play a critical role.

Philip Tetlock convincingly advises that we should consider expert advice with caution. Over a 20-year period, Tetlock followed the forecasts of 284 experts who were professional predictors of political and economic trends. He asked them to rate the probability of three different possible outcomes: no change in the current situation or either an increase or decrease in a factor like economic growth. He discovered that the experts with many years of experience and Ph.D.s were roughly as accurate as dart-throwing monkeys.[27] This is in no way meant to disparage the advice of all experts; after all, forecasting the future is a difficult thing. However, it is sensible to view most prognostications cautiously.

In his book *Streetlights and Shadows*, the psychologist Gary Klein, states the following:

> I am saddened to see ineffective decision-support systems that are designed in accordance with ideology rather than observation. If we try to balance the human as hazard model with the human as hero model, and to balance the automatic, intuitive system with the reflective, analytical system, we should have more of a chance to create decision-support systems that will get used.[28]

The tools and processes discussed in the rest of this book will attempt to just that: combine both the intuitive and analytical to provide us with the best possible decision.

1.1.8 Types of Decision Making

Hoch and Kunreuther propose three different levels from which decision making can be viewed:[29]

- **Normative:** The normative approach holds, for example, that we would be better served by making decisions based on rationality.

- **Descriptive:** The descriptive level describes what we actually observe about how decisions are made.

- **Prescriptive:** Prescriptive recommendations focus on improving decision making.

Much decision science research and work is tied to formal mathematical models. Recently, however, cognitive approaches to decision making have been a focus. This discussion adopts a *prescriptive* approach to our evaluation of the various factors that impact decision making and the technologies that can influence desirable outcomes.

1.2 Rise of the Machines: Advanced Analytics and Decision Making

According to Gartner, Inc., the term *advanced analytics* is defined as follows:[30]

> As analysis of structured and content (such as text, images, video, voice) data using sophisticated quantitative methods (such as statistics, descriptive and predictive data mining, simulation, and optimization) to produce insights that traditional approaches to BI such as query and reporting are unlikely to discover. It is frequently applied to make decisions, solve business problems and identify opportunities by providing better forecasts, causal understanding, pattern identification, process and resource optimization, and assisting with scenario planning process.

The challenge is that although substantial gains wait, very few firms actually utilize advanced analytics. Only 13% of organizations utilize predictive analytics, and only 3% use prescriptive analytics, such as optimization and simulation.[31] To this list, I want to add *actionable recommendations,* such as provided by machine learning and expert systems.

Recently, the focus on HCM metrics has gone a long way toward establishing the relationships between variables of interest (for example, training initiatives) and performance outcomes (for example, employee turnover by division).[32] Advanced analytics provides a deepening of the tools associated with business intelligence, with a focus on predicting and prescribing the optimal course of action. These techniques are increasingly being used in functions like operations, finance, and marketing and can have the same impact within human resources.

According to Gartner, this will matter.[33]

Pervasive, advanced analytics will become necessary for leading organizations that want to gain competitive advantage.

The explosion of data volume, and its variety and velocity, will enable new, high-value advanced analytic insights and use cases.

Lack of skills will be a critical inhibitor to adoption and deriving value from advanced analytics.

Embedding collaboration and social capabilities in advanced analytic applications will facilitate higher quality and more transparent decision making.

There is an ever-increasing need for data scientists—those who understand statistics, computer science, and data modeling and analysis. More effective HR decisions can be made when these skills are used to assist with the full spectrum of HR tools.

1.2.1 Advanced Analytics

As mentioned previously, we can improve our decision making. Metrics and analytics have long been used to assist decision making, and as computing power increases (along with our understanding of behavior), our tools are becoming more powerful as we develop models that more accurately predict outcomes.

Figure 1.1 provides an overview of a hierarchy of analytics. Level I is an organization's use of basic metrics to obtain information such as headcount, employee turnover, and even some simple statistics such as the use of means and averages. Next is Level II, which is characterized by correlations. This consists of determining whether and when variables move relative to one another. For example, as employee morale goes up, what happens to employee turnover? Of course, correlations do not mean causation; however, they do suggest a possible relationship. Level III shows a focus on establishing causation and on predictions of what will happen next (anything from who will make a good employee to whether a specific payment package will promote the intended organizational outcomes).

Advanced analytics can aid in establishing causation, which is generally thought of as the holy grail of analytics. That is, does the intervention we put in place have a direct impact on the bottom line? For instance, does the new compensation approach increase employee productivity, reduce employee turnover, and ultimately impact sales and profitability? This can then be used not only to justify expenditures but also to make determinations about what policy, practice, or intervention is advantageous to use in the future.

Advanced analytics can be thought of in two parts. Part one attempts to predict what will occur. As discussed in the previous section, this requires a broad understanding of how individuals and groups will react. Part two, and the primary focus of this book, is about optimization. The focus here is not about what a decision *will* be, but rather what it *should* be.

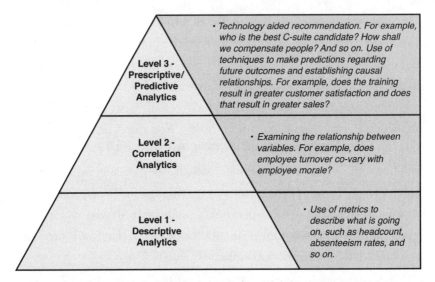

Figure 1.1   Hierarchy of analytics

It is a good thing that these tools are becoming more available, because according to a 2010 survey by IBM, there is a real need for HCM decisions to move toward higher levels of prediction and causation.[34] That survey found that advanced analytics were rarely used for activities such as evaluating workforce performance, retaining valued talent, and developing future leaders. Nowhere, on any of these HR issues reviewed, did more than a quarter of the organizations actually engage in advanced analytics. One of the least used analytical processes is the use of collaboration across the organization. Only 5% of the firms interviewed used advanced analytics along with collaboration and knowledge sharing.

HR has nothing to feel bad about. It is estimated that only 3% of firms use any form of advanced analytics. However, it is projected that the use of analytics will grow substantially over the coming years.[35] This book covers each of these three perspectives of decision making:[36]

- **Descriptive:** What happened and what is happening?

- **Predictive:** What will happen? What might happen?

- **Prescriptive:** What should happen? What is the best course of action?

1.2.2 Predicting Outcomes

Recently, the Sundem-Tierney equation has been updated. You may be wondering what exactly the Sundem-Tierney equation is used for. Basically, it predicts how long the marriages of celebrities will last. As one of the authors proclaims, tongue in cheek, "One of great unsolved mysteries in social science."[37]

The Sundem-Tierney Celebrity Marriage Longevity Equation

$$\sqrt{\frac{NYT}{ENQ}} \frac{(Ah + Aw)}{(Sc + 5)} Md \left[\frac{Md}{(Md + 2)} \right] T^2$$

Where:

NYT = The number of times the wife's name been mentioned in the *New York Times*

ENQ = The number of times the wife's name has been mentioned in the *National Enquirer*

Ah = Age in years of the husband

Aw = Age in years of the wife

Md = Number of months the couple dated before marriage

Sc = Number of scantily clad photos from the top five photos found during a Google image search of her name

T = Time in years for which you want to calculate the percentage chance the couple will still be married

This equation represents a revision of the old equation, and it turns out that this one is a much more robust predictor of the duration of celebrity marriages. For example, the equation accurately predicts that Jennifer Lopez's marriage to Ojani Noa (her first husband, a relationship that most people don't even know about) would not last very long (it lasted 13 months), but it predicts a 71% chance that Prince William and Kate Middleton will make it 15 years or longer.

Many become nervous when they hear things like "model building" or "optimization," but this does not need to be so intimidating. There is nothing intimidating about listing the factors that go into making the best decision. Getting all the best and required data might not always be especially easy, but determining the *determinants* (the factors influencing an outcome) can actually be rather fun and interesting. Take, for example, the following equation; it is attempting to determine the likelihood of marital bliss. By Robyn Dawes, this model predicts the likelihood of the survival of a marriage.[38]

Frequency of Lovemaking – Frequency of Quarrels

See, nothing at all boring about predictive modeling. As you might imagine, having a negative number associated with this equation is not a good thing. Because of the availability of the necessary data, predictions such as these are becoming more and more common and found across many facets of life. Predicting compatibility is the task organizations such as Match.com and eHarmony attempt to do. Dawes formula is a simple one that essentially attempts to serve the same function as the ones developed by these dating services. They are both attempting to identify a list of factors that will predict the success of relationships. In the case of eHarmony and Match.com, this also consists of information on emotional, cognitive, and social attributes, physical activity, personality characteristics, education, geography, and so on.

One more:

Runs Created = (Hits + Walks) × Total Bases / (At Bats + Walks)

Some of you might recognize this formula. William James, the founder of sabermetrics, developed it. If this is not familiar to you, maybe you remember the book *Moneyball,* by Michael Lewis, or the movie by the same name starring Brad Pitt. James's sabermetrics is the underlying approach used to predict success at getting on base, and this is exactly what the formula predicts: a hitter's ability to get on base. It did not worry about exactly how he got there. As a matter of fact, the formula takes into consideration those who walk as well as those who get hits.[39]

Making predictions is something that we do all the time. Will a stock price go up or down? Will your friends get married? Will this person make a good employee or a good executive? What kind of professional experiences will assist them in becoming better employees?

Within the broad area of decision support systems, a variety of different models are used to aid in decision making.[40] The relevant variables when "modeling" HCM decisions include all those factors that influence the outcome you are interested in. For example, what might be some of the causes of employee turnover? This decision will be influenced by, among other things, a number of the following factors:

- Employee morale and satisfaction

- Labor market conditions

- Relationship with direct reports

Another example is workforce planning, which seeks to accurately forecast future employment needs. Again, a number of factors may influence the best decision about the type and number of employees needed, including the following:

- Business strategy and objectives

- Current workforce quantity and competencies

- Required workforce quantity and competencies

In later chapters, we will evaluate factors influencing the ideal job candidate for your situation and the optimal compensation structure. Determining these factors is where expert knowledge and experience comes in, and when these are combined with the right analytics, you are on your way to making much better decisions.

1.2.3 Improper Linear Models: Combining Expert Intuition with Analytics

The work of Robyn Dawes provides an excellent justification and argument for the use of expert expertise combined with the use of advanced analytics. Analytics can be used to develop a comprehensive list of factors that ultimately promote performance, or make a good employee, or any number of different decisions, and the experts can use their expertise to develop the weightings for the various factors.

In his article "The Robust Beauty of Improper Linear Models in Decision Making," Dawes remarkably concluded that a simple algorithm is accurate enough to compete with regression analysis and, frankly, much better than the opinion of an expert. Consider, for example, the *Apgar test*. In 1953, Dr. Virginia Apgar, an anesthesiologist, was asked how she would assess the health of a newborn. She wrote down five variables (respiration, reflex, muscle tone, color, and heart rate) and assigned a score of 0, 1, or 2 depending on the strength of the variable. A baby with a score of 4 or less needed immediate attention, and a baby with a score of 8 or more was pink, crying, and good to go. This simple algorithm has certainly saved the lives of thousands of babies over the years.[41]

Yes, this is a simple algorithm, but identifying which variables are important is not so simple. Picking the important variable that predicted newborn health was done by someone who had very deep practical experience and research. Dr. Virginia Apgar was born in 1909 in Westfield, New Jersey, and was educated at Mount Holyoke College and Columbia University College of Physicians and Surgeons (CUCPS), where she graduated in 1933 and finished her residency in 1937. She went on to become the first woman to become a full professor at CUCPS, in 1949. Dr. Apgar had 20 years of experience around newborns when she developed her test. She had considerable *expert* knowledge through observation, study, experience, research, and practical experience to establish those five variables. Could there be other (better) ones? Maybe. Could, perhaps, respiration be the most important and color the least at predicting the well-being of the newborn? These are exactly the types of questions that deep analytics can answer.

This approach is further supported by Stephen Hoch in the summary of his chapter, "Combing Models with Intuition to Improve Decisions":[42]

> Most decisions have three stages: (1) variable identification, (2) variable valuation, and (3) information integration into an overall evaluation. Experts are good at the first two stages but are plagued by inconsistency in stage three. By outsourcing stage three to a mechanical model, the quality of decisions can be enhanced. By carefully combining human experts, statistical models, and new data-mining tools, we can improve the quality of forecasts and other decisions.[43]

We'll be using this exact approach when modeling our decisions: an expert determining the importance of factors coupled with analytics.

1.2.4 Artificial Intelligence and Machine Learning

What exactly is meant by the term *artificial intelligence* (AI) garners a significant amount of discussion. Machine learning and expert systems are both forms of AI. There is also natural language and the neural nets and other AI tools. As the name suggests, natural language refers to the capability of machines to understand and act on spoken language. Neural nets are computer systems that mimic the human brain. For our purposes, I will focus on machine learning and sophisticated expert systems (sometime referred to as Deep Q&A expert systems). Both have substantial scope for assisting with the decision making within HCM and elsewhere.

According to Yaser S. Abu-Mostafa, a Professor of electrical engineering and computer science at Cal Tech and the co-author of the book *Learning from Data*, at its most basic, machine learning can be defined as follows:

> At its simplest, machine learning algorithms take an existing data set, comb through it for patterns, then use these patterns to generate predictions about the future.[44]

Machine learning has been utilized within a number of different functions, including finance, marketing, and operations (and in HR, but less so). It is generally associated with the ability, as the name implies, to learn (mostly through trial and error). An example is in gaming settings, where the system can learn by playing the game over and over. This is one of the reasons that machine learning can be used effectively for chess or Jeopardy!; they are games that are repeated. Within HR, there is also repetition; we hire computer programmers again and again, we design and deliver compensation repeatedly, and we put our high-potential employees through executive development programs. All of these activities can be refined through utilizing machine learning.

The following list describes a few instances of when machine learning can be applied to HR decisions:

- Identify professional experience, educational attainment, personal characteristics, and other life experiences associated with superior job performance

- Use social media to obtain information on the success of a specific recruitment approach

- Identify factors associated with voluntary turnover of high-potential candidates

- Predict future workforce skills and quantity

The applications of machine learning are many, but there are also potential drawbacks. Machine learning relies primarily on the use of an algorithm as it trolls through a dataset looking for instance the "ideal" candidate or the ideal pay package. Again, according to Abu-Mostafa,[45] it is not always easy to actually name or identify the attributes that have been identified. In addition, many decisions associated with HCM may need to be explicitly defined or backed out of. An employee (or potentially the courts) may question how a specific decision was arrived at. This might not always be easy to determine when using machine learning. Machine learning tends to use algorithms to do the work. Algorithms are a predetermined set of factors that need to be evaluated to arrive at some required output. An example is calculating payroll; this takes into consideration hours worked, overtime, tax, and other deductions.

Whereas machine learning focuses on the use of algorithms, expert systems utilize heuristic approaches. Heuristic approaches generally follow a set of rules to arrive at some conclusion or recommendation. Expert systems make it possible to see how a decision was made.

1.3 Human and Machine: The Ideal Decision-Making Team

We are in luck because machines happen to be very good at exactly what we are not so good at. Gartner, the information technology consulting and research firm, produces a series of research notes that cover a wide range of topics related to information technology and associated topics and disciplines. The company occasionally issues what they refer to as "maverick" research, which is research that pushes the technological and social envelope on a topic. One such research note, "Judgment Day, or Why We Should Let Machines Automate Decision Making,"[46] was written by Nigel Rayner. They believe that we are at a point at which more and more decisions will be automated and the decisions taken by machines will be better than ones made by humans.

In their recent book *Race Against the Machine,* Erik Brynjolfsson and Andrew McAfee of MIT provide some insight into the question of our relationship to technology. There has long been a question about whether technology will replace us or complement us. This is a question that has been around since the first machine was built. The position taken in *Race Against the Machine* is that our decisions can be far superior if we leverage those aspects of machines that *complement* our own facilities. Brynjolfsson and McAfee discuss the 1997 loss of Garry Kasparov to IBM's Deep Blue supercomputer. The media seized on to the win by Deep Blue; discussed much less was the fact that the best chess champions were actually teams of humans using computers. According to Kasparov, a strong human player using a standard laptop was able to beat Hydra, a supercomputer designed for chess.[47] CEOs find that data-driven decisions provide the greatest potential for long-term value creation.[48] This really is the crux of the matter: developing and utilizing technologies that compensate for our weaknesses and accentuate our strengths.

Are some HCM decisions best addressed through advanced analytics? The fact is that these new and developing tools could aid with nearly all decisions. Table 1.2 describes some of the important HCM decisions and how advanced analytics can assist.

Table 1.2 HCM Decision Framework

HCM Decision	Challenges to Optimal Decision Making	Advanced Analytical Tool
Alignment with organizational objectives	Tremendous variation of situations and potential policies and practices	Machine learning/expert systems
Workforce planning	Broad scope of pertinent information	Simulation and predictive analytics
		Machine learning/expert systems
Selection	Biases	Predictive analytics
		Machine learning/expert systems
Performance management	Biases	Predictive analytics
		Machine learning/expert systems
Compensation	Biases	Machine learning/expert systems
	Large data sources	
Collaborative decision making	Data overload	Predictive analytics/expert systems

1.3.1 A Word About AI Tools

A number of different AI software applications are available from various AI vendors. In addition, many different open source and commercially available tools can assist with decision making. I am going to be primarily using a sophisticated expert system called Expert Maker, which includes a broad range of AI tools. You can find these tools on this book's website: DecisionAnalyticsInc.com.

Depending on your level of interest, you might want to consider a number of open source and commercially available tools, including

Python, R, Octave, WEKA, MATLAB, Apache Hadoop, and vendors (including the usual suspects SAS, IBM, Oracle, and SAP) that are developing ever-more sophisticated AI tools in their business intelligence and other offerings. In addition, some smaller companies and start-ups are doing very interesting things. I profile a few in later chapters. There is much more to say about this, so I encourage you to visit the website (DecisionAnalyicsInc.com) to find more information. I also strongly recommend that if you do not know how to code, learn. There are great online resources available to help you with this (Codeacademy, Code/Racer, MIT OpenCourseWare, Coursera, among others).

2

Collaboration, Cooperation, and Reciprocity

2.1 Human Nature and Human Science

Some of you may remember the events of January 28, 1986, and the image of the space shuttle Challenger streaking skyward only to disappear in a cloud of white exhaust, errant boosters, and falling debris. In the coming months and years, much of the blame for the disaster was placed on the decision-making process at NASA and the subcontractor Morton Thiokol.[1] It was well known that the O-rings tended to become rigid and unseal at low temperatures, even temperatures found in Florida. The launch-time temperature was 30 degrees Fahrenheit, well below the safe launch threshold. The O-ring failure may have led directly to the disintegration of the shuttle, but the actual cause of the disaster was a decision-making process that ignored the facts, did not involve and listen to those with critical information, and had a "culture" that rewarded launch over safety.

Roger Boisjoly was an engineer with Morton Thiokol who knew there was a high probability of a catastrophic failure of the O-rings. Six months prior to the disaster, he sent a memo to his superiors warning them of potential problems. On the day before the disaster, Boisjoly and four others engineers attempted to warn their superiors about the dangerously low temperatures and the probability of an O-ring failure. They were disregarded by Morton Thiokol's general manager, who told them to "Take off your engineering hats and put on your management hats."[2]

Mr. Boisjoly reported his firm's failings and paid a heavy price for his whistleblowing and subsequent lawsuits against Thiokol and NASA. One colleague at Thiokol threatened to drop off his children at Boisjoly's doorstep if they lost their jobs.[3] NASA was also dismissive. The only NASA official to show Boisjoly any support at the time was astronaut Sally Ride, who served on the commission examining the tragedy. However, Boisjoly recovered and went on to speak at more than 300 universities about data and ethical decision making. NASA also made sweeping changes and became a model of analytics, collaboration, and participative decision making. Launch decisions were made based on the best available data and only after input from everyone involved, including the astronauts flying the mission.[4]

The story of the Challenger disaster makes a poignant and critical point: The best data and the most sophisticated algorithms and artificial intelligence (AI) technology on the planet are not going to make a bit of difference if the *facts* are ignored, *and,* just as critically, if the culture (that is, the incentives and decision-making structures) rewards and promotes non-value-maximizing behaviors. How do we structure our companies and decisions to reduce the possibility of the wrong decision and increase the probability of making the right ones? How do we develop organizations where people and teams with critical information are heard, listened to, encouraged, and rewarded for speaking up? What technologies can assist with making the organization more collaborative and with getting the right information to decision makers?

Not all decisions may be so impactful as to lead to the loss of life; however, the wrong decisions will almost certainly lead to the loss of optimal organizational performance.

2.1.1 Reciprocity and Fairness

When I first moved from the Midwest to the East Coast, I had a "bias" that everyone in the region was going to be in a big rush and generally rude and aggressive. Soon after arriving, though, one of the first things I noticed was that people would hold doors open for me, sometimes for what I considered to be an inordinately long period of time. I decided that perhaps these East Coast types were not all that rude and rushed, and I happily joined the ranks of door holders. Recently, I was sharing my East Coast door-holding observations with a friend and learned that she had found the same thing. However, she also noticed that some were gaming the door-holding goodwill and waiting for people to get the door for them. She suggested that when I find myself at a glass door, I see whether the person on the other side has stopped and is waiting for me to get the door for them. I live in an apartment complex with glass doors, so this was easy to do. I started observing fellow residents' and guests' door-holding habits. Whereas most people went out of their way to get the door, a few would wait (a long time) for people to get the door for them. This was not expectant mothers, the elderly, or even people carrying a ton of stuff. Instead, they were generally completely able bodied and otherwise-unencumbered folks who were generally younger and less encumbered than I. So, when I approached the door and could see one of the door-holding gamers waiting for me to get the door for them, I would stop, smile, and wait to see who blinked. Because they realized someone was on to them, they would quickly get the door.

Before you start thinking I am being rather petty, turns out I am far from the only one who is concerned with fairness, reciprocity, and equality. As it happens, these characteristics are fundamental to who we are. As a matter of fact, it is hypothesized that reciprocity and cooperation may in part drive our very evolution. Harvard biologist and mathematician Michael Nowak stated the following in a seminal article:

Thus, we might add "natural cooperation" as a third fundamental principle of evolution beside mutation and natural selection.[5]

The article evaluates five different reasons for the existence of cooperation: kin selection, direct reciprocity, indirect reciprocity, networked reciprocity, and group selection. It appears that even at an evolutionary level cooperation may promote greater "fitness" when compared to a competitive model.

2.1.2 Selfish, Greedy, Lazy, and Dishonest

A long-held assumption within economics is that humans are fundamentally a greedy, lazy, and selfish species prone to lying and cheating.[6] You might think that I am overstating the case for dramatic effect, but I assure you that I am not. Much of this evolved from Adam Smith's "invisible hand" and the notion that each of us seeking our own self-interest will ultimately lead to better outcomes for everyone. Adam Smith might not have been promoting the kind of self-centered "greed is good" that his notion evolved into, but over the years it is difficult to argue that it has not led to a rather one-sided view of human nature, at least within economics.

This negative underlying assumption about our nature has had a big effect on the way in which incentive contracts and the employment relationship has been theorized and ultimately implemented within organizations. Managers sometimes go to extreme lengths to monitor workers because otherwise, of course, they goof off all day. The surveillance in place at some organizations can be downright Orwellian. Even if your every move is not being monitored, in many places, the "command and control" work environment is alive and well. In addition, tournament-based incentive contracts are largely if not exclusively focused on individual accomplishments, often providing no incentive to share potentially useful information, and sometimes even providing an incentive to sabotage the work of others. So, what on earth are the 3Ms and the Googles of this world doing when they allow their employees one day per week to work on whatever they want? Clearly, from the perspective of economic self-interest, giving employees a day off each week to pursue their own interests is the same as giving them, well, the day off. Of course, if this policy did not exist at 3M and Google, we might not have scotch tape and Gmail.

2.1.3 Human Nature 2.0

One of the most prolific and influential economists working today is Ernst Fehr at the University of Zurich. He and his collaborators have had the same impact undoing the fundamental belief that we are all primarily greedy and selfish that Kahneman and his co-authors had on unraveling the notion of rationality. Fehr and others have closely examined notions of altruism, reciprocity, cooperation, and fairness and have found that we are actually a very unselfish and helpful species.[7] Who knew, right? He and others have gone further and applied these findings to the way in which the employment contract is structured. Taken in light of their work, the 3M and Google model does not appear to be so absurd. As a matter of fact, if you hire the right people and have the right incentives and culture in place, you may be able to give employees two days off a week to work on their own projects. (Imagine what they might come up with.)

We are actually quite good at self-regulation. The political scientist Elinor Ostrom, another recipient of the Nobel Prize in Economics, has shot holes in the long-held notion of "the tragedy of the commons." This concept suggests that when left to our own devices, we will exploit a common resource until it is devastated. However, clearly it is hardly in a fisherman's self-interest to decimate the fish population or ranchers to use up all the water. Turns out the use of the commons in not so tragic; exhausting all common assets just does not always happen. An example is water rights in Arizona and fishing rights in Massachusetts. Both have been successfully self-regulated, with the resource remaining intact.

Again, all you have to do is look around. Humans clearly do not always make decisions rationally, and humans are also empathetic, altruistic, concerned about being treated fairly, and also want to see others treated fairly. Need further proof? Look no further than April 15, 2013, the day of the Boston Marathon bombings. One of the first things you will notice if you look at photographs or videos of the attack is that many, many people are running *toward* the site of the bomb detonations. This included many first responders; however, it also included many normal citizens. There is nothing rational or self-interested about running toward the site of bomb blasts. The rational response by a rational self-interested agent would be to turn and run like hell in the opposite direction. Two bombs had just detonated, dramatically increasing the probability of there being more. Nonetheless, a few moments after the explosions, so many people were assisting it was difficult to even see the victims.

2.1.4 Fierce Cooperation

When people hear the word *cooperation,* they sometimes envision people sitting around in a circle sharing, actively listening, and generally affirming what others are saying. While all of these conditions may well be a part of the cooperative process, cooperation and cooperative behaviors are not always affirming. Take, for example, the notion of reciprocity: I will look out for you, but you also need to look out for me; if you don't, I may call you on it.

As with many of the topics that really engage me, I came to the notion of reciprocity and mutual monitoring largely through the back door. Maya Kroumova and I were interested in the impact firm size would have on the effectiveness of broadly distributed stock options.[8] Agency theory would strongly predict that the smaller the firm the more likely they would be to have an impact on firm performance. The idea being that in a small firm—say 30, 100, 500 employees—it is much more reasonable to expect that employees would think that their actions would ultimately impact the share price, consequently providing more motivation for them to work longer and harder. What we found was that firm size did not matter at all. Small, medium, even large firms all benefited from the use of broadly distributed stock options. We were surprised by this finding and tested and retested the data only to find the same thing. At the time, the finding did not make a tremendous amount of sense to us, so we suggested more research be conducted to evaluate what actual mechanisms were at work. We promptly sent the paper out to a number of journals, and it was promptly rejected by all of them (though you can find it at SSRN.com).

We continued to work and rework the paper trying to figure out what was going on, and then one day noticed that a number of behavioral economics were referencing the paper in their work and using it to support the notion of mutual monitoring.[9] It started to make sense; at the organizational level, one of the reasons that reciprocity works is because, mixed with the right incentives, employees have an incentive to keep an eye on one another. If your rewards depend on the contribution of others (as they do for everyone holding shares in the same company), you are more likely to call someone on it if he or she is not being productive. What we found was that both small and large firms did better. If this was the mechanism at work, size would not matter; as a matter of fact, the bigger the firm would be more likely to benefit from shared rewards like broad-based stock options, because having everyone keeping an eye on everyone else was much more efficient than other forms of monitoring.

The evidence is becoming more clear on this; mutual monitoring and reciprocity is more efficient than hiring many managers to monitor the workforce, or putting in place expensive surveillance equipment. This is not to suggest that developing a culture of collaboration is cost free, just that the alternative is often more costly.

2.1.5 Collaboration

Those of you who saw the movie *A Beautiful Mind*[10] may remember the scene where Russell Crowe (who played John Nash, the 1994 recipient of the Nobel Prize in Economics) imagines a scene meant to depict an aspect of game theory. In the scene, five young men in a bar spot five women, one of whom is exceptionally attractive; the other four are merely very attractive. The five make a beeline for the exceptionally attractive woman and all vie for her affections. The attractive woman is perturbed by this and annoyed that her friends are being ignored, so she ignores the men. Her friends are equally angry at being slighted, so when the young men turn their attention to the friends, they rebuke their advances. The five men decide their best strategy is to work together. Instead of going after the exceptionally attractive woman, they head directly to the friends. Everyone hits it off, and so by working together, they are each individually able to improve their utility.

The scene is meant to depict a core notion of game theory, which states that sometimes our individual utility is enhanced when we collude or work together. This is contrary to the standard neoclassical view that essentially states we should all pursue our own self-interest and from this the most efficient outcomes will result. Clearly, the notion of collusion here is used in a good sense: working together, sharing information that facilities better decision making. An increasing body of work outside of economics also supports this notion of cooperation over individual utility maximization. There are examples of this in the natural sciences, as well. The biologist E. O. Wilson found that when it comes to cooperative behaviors, groups that learned to cooperate among themselves were much more likely to survive and prosper.[11] There is substantial and growing evidence again, across many different disciplines and functions, that the more we can work together, the better the performance outcomes. Academia is one place that has benefited greatly from the free collaboration and the free flow of ideas and information. The open source software movement, Wikipedia, and all the other wikis are all excellent examples of collective collaboration. Many of us benefit from this kind of collaboration, and many of us also contribute to these efforts.

In addition, substantial and interesting work is being done on the wisdom of crowds and collective intelligence; we are simply smarter together than alone. Thomas Malone, the founding director of MIT Center for Collective Intelligence, believes that organizations need to fundamentally change because all the new technologies have resulted in a change not in the production technology, but rather in the coordination technology.[12] These coordination technologies include the technologies that we will be discussing that promote better decision making.

2.1.6 Hard Wired to Share What We Know

It's official now: It is highly unlikely that a *Planet of the Apes* scenario will ever exist here on Earth. Turns out that an undervalued aspect of what sets humans apart from all other species is our tendency to share our knowledge. Our willingness, even desire, to share what we know is referred to by anthropologists as *ratcheting*.[13] And this is no small thing; it might be one of the most important qualities that allowed humans to advance and thrive. Our tendency to share what we know may have provided us with an insurmountable advantage when it comes to competing with all other species. Universities excel as places where information is shared broadly, but many organizations are not good at sharing information (although there are notable exceptions).

Knowledge management has been around for some time and has a mixed record of success.[14] Much of this mixed success relates to actually getting people to utilize the systems in place, and it appears that incentives are the problem (and organizations being locked into these systems). A sophisticated enterprise content or knowledge management system will go to waste if the right incentives and organization does not support it. The organization consists of a number of elements, including content management software systems and a culture of collaboration and information sharing.[15] There has to be an incentive to share information and an incentive to collaborate. The system itself is just one small piece of the puzzle.

This notion of reciprocity or reciprocal altruism is also well understood within cultural anthropology literature. We are much more likely to be generous with those who are generous with us, and the same applies on the organizational level. The topic of knowledge management is a broad one, and our focus here is on how collaborative decision making and how you can use new and developing technologies to assist in decision making. One of the fastest-growing segments of knowledge management is the use of collaborative software systems to assist with decision making. An ever-growing body of literature across many different disciplines provides support for the efficiencies of collaboration.[16]

2.1.7 Collective Intelligence

Some of the better known examples of the utilization of collective intelligence include Wikipedia and InnoCentive. InnoCentive is a web-based service that outsources companies' research problems, inviting solutions from the web community. Good ideas are rewarded with cash prizes. Of course, this is one of the reasons democracy works as well as it does. It is impossible for any one person to see the whole picture, but collectively we often get it right (maybe not right away, but eventually).

Individually, we are prone to make decisions that are susceptible to all sorts of individual biases and environmental factors. However, when we gather information from a variety of information sources, we are much more likely to make good decisions. Unfortunately, a number of historical and environmental factors paint democracy in the workplace as somehow being subversive.[17] Many strongly support democracy at a national level but not at the organizational level. This is an unfortunate fact, because like our desire to share what we know, getting involved in our organizations should be encouraged (as should expressing what we think).

2.1.8 Asymmetric or Private Information

The core reason that employee involvement and cooperation and collaboration are so critical relates to the notion of asymmetric or private information. There was a time in my own career when many organizations put in place employee participation programs, but primarily as window dressing. As you can guess, they were not especially effective. However, if done right, employee participation programs can serve two equally critical functions. They can serve to better engage employees, and they can serve to get the best possible information to those who are making decisions.

The term used in the economic literature to describe this type of information is *asymmetric information* or *private information,* and the fact of its existence is why organizations should go to tremendous lengths to ensure that their employees are engaged, motivated, have a strong incentive to share information, and (probably most important) that they *do not leave.* Once you have found someone who is an especially good fit with your organization, you want to go to great lengths to ensure that he or she stays. The information they have at their disposal, and whether they decide to share and act on this information, has the potential to tremendously increase the probability of organizational success.

Asymmetric information simply means that only I know what I know. Only the individual knows how hard he or she can work, for example, or whether he or she has any good ideas about how to improve the production process. If they are in direct contact with the customer, they also have significant information about how customers like to be treated and about customer preferences. If the employees are in direct contact with the products being built, they also have access to tremendously valuable information about the production process and the quality of the products. If they are responsible for new product development, they certainly have a great amount of information about great new products. Not leveraging this information is like organizations leaving money on the table, but many organizations do just that.

2.1.9 Game Theory 101

This section discusses the classic example of the prisoners' dilemma, often used to explain game theory. You can see from the following example that it is the self-interest of both prisoners to hope the other prisoner confesses. However, it is not in either prisoner's self-interest to confess. It is unlikely that either prisoner will convince the other to confess. So in this case, the best possible outcome is one of working together or cooperating. There will be a cost, but it will not be as high as if they both choose to go it alone, as shown in Figure 2.1.

Individual 2

Individual 1	Cooperate (remain silent)	Defect (confess)
Cooperate (remain silent)	2 years in jail 2 years in jail	4 years in jail 1 year in jail
Defect (confess)	1 year in jail 4 years in jail	3 years in jail 3 years in jail

Figure 2.1 The prisoners' dilemma

Collaboration and shared decision making work because by setting shared rewards people eventually figure out that it is in their self-interest to work together. One aspect of game theory that human capital management (HCM) has direct bearing on is employee turnover. The greater the employee turnover, the less likely that a cooperative culture will emerge. This argues that there should be a premium placed on ensuring that key contributors stay with the organization.

2.2 The Power of Collaboration: The Scandinavian Model

Each year, a number of business publications list the best countries or cities to do business. The cover of a recent issue of *The Economist* magazine announced "The next supermodel" while showing a picture of a Viking (a Viking with his nose turned up). The subtitle under the picture of the skeptical-looking Viking was "Why the world should look at the Nordic countries." This edition of *The Economist* includes a 14-page special report that provides a number of insights into the Scandinavian model. Table 2.1 pretty much says it all. Of course, keep in mind that organizations are not countries. Also keep in mind, though, that a number of businesses are bigger than some countries. There are lessons we can extrapolate to our organizations.

The argument people make about the Scandinavian model is that these countries are relatively homogenous and so this kind of shared-destiny philosophy is more likely to thrive. This might well be true; but even so, our most diverse organizations are certainly much less diverse than any one of these countries. So, if these characteristics are associated with their success, organizations should almost certainly benefit from them. Another defining characteristic of these countries is they have some of the lowest wage inequality of any of the major economies. This is certainly a large part of their success and is something that organizations can learn from. The power of everyone sharing in the prosperity of the organization is a powerful motivator and means of engaging the workforce.

Table 2.1   International Economic and Social Comparisons

Overall Rank	Country Prosperity	Global Competitive	Ease of Business	Global Innov	Corruption	Human Develop
1	Sweden	4	13	2	4	10	3
2	Denmark	12	5	7	1	16	2
3	Finland	3	11	4	1	22	7
4	Norway	15	6	14	7	1	1
5	Switzerland	1	28	1	6	11	9
6	New Zealand	23	3	13	1	5	5
7	Singapore	2	1	3	5	26	19
8	United States	7	4	10	19	4	12
9	Netherlands	5	31	6	9	3	8
10	Canada	14	17	12	9	6	6
11	Hong Kong	9	2	8	14	13	18
12	Australia	20	10	23	7	2	4
13	Britain	8	7	5	17	28	13
14	Germany	6	20	15	13	9	14
15	Ireland	27	15	9	25	7	10

2.2.1 What Kinds of Organizations Could Benefit from a High Degree of Collaboration?

The short answer is pretty much every one of them. Based on case studies of organizations that do an especially good job with collaboration, knowledge-intensive organizations such as consultancies and other organizations do an especially good job of sharing the intellectual capital of their members. Oddly, although a substantial degree of collaboration exists *between* academics across institutions, there is generally not as much collaboration *within* academic institutions. Part of the problem with academic institutions is a tendency for each of the schools or departments to work as silos (something the private sector works hard to eliminate, with varying degrees of success).[18]

However, certain types of organizations would benefit to a greater degree than some others. For instance, knowledge-intensive firms that do not have collaborative systems in place are losing out on a substantial amount of potentially productivity and profit-enhancing information.

However, it is not only knowledge intensive firms with employees that are highly educated and skilled that can benefit from collaborative initiatives.

In fact, though, organizations can have a high degree of *information capital,* and this may exist in organizations where few employees have formal educational qualifications but that have access to a high degree of competitive information based on direct contact with customers, the products and production process, and the innovative process.

2.2.2 The Benefits of Collaboration

Nearly everywhere you look there is an increasing focus on collaboration. Knowledge-intensive firms have adopted open office plans that promote the free flow of information. Michael Bloomberg did this at Bloomberg LLC, and this is also the way in which he structured

City Hall upon becoming mayor of New York. Firms have adopted a tremendous number of knowledge management software for the organization. There is a growing body of evidence that the better we are at collaboration, the better we are at coming up with great products and first-rate service.

2.2.3 The Bottom-Line Impact of Participative Decision Making

The question here is really this: Why bother with collaborative decisions making? Doesn't this just slow things down? This is another topic I have researched and one that indicates that there are gains associated with greater involvement. In companies where collaboration is the norm, you are likely to get much greater investment (engagement by employees and stakeholders). A significant body of research indicates a strong link between employee involvement and the ultimate success of the enterprise.

Greater performance outcomes are associated with greater collaboration for a number of reasons. An engaged culture is critical to successful collaboration, and advanced analytics can assist with this. In addition to the substantial benefits associated with having employee feel more engaged, substantial efficiencies are associated with the flow of information. Those who are in direct contact with the products being built, with the services being delivered, with the customers—these people have access to asymmetric information, and without question, developing collaboration systems will lead to much greater and sustained competitive advantage.

Substantial research indicates a positive economic impact from collaboration. However, executives (or a small group of executives) often make big decisions based mostly on the information they have readily at hand. As discussed in Chapter 1, "Challenges and Opportunities with Optimal Decision Making and How Advanced Analytics Can Help," decisions made this way often lead to outcomes that are far from optimal. Many decisions might be much better if they included as much information as possible. Collaborative decision-making systems are a vehicle to get the right information to the right people, who can then make the right decisions.

2.2.4 Organizational Culture

Considerable changes need to be made in organizations to make them places where employees are fully engaged and have an incentive to share what they know and are intent to stay (and so not spend time looking for the next job). Building such an *organizational culture* is worth the effort.

I have never liked the term organizational culture. This admission will get me in trouble with friends who conduct research on the topic, but it always struck me as simply too vague. For instance, with regard to the Challenger disaster, I recall hearing that a problem with the organizational culture at NASA ultimately led to the disaster. Honestly, to say that the culture caused the disaster doesn't tell me much of anything. What actually led to the disaster were a very identifiable decision-making structures and specific incentives.

Essentially, corporate culture boils down to who does what and how do we motivate for productivity. All the activities associated with HCM revolve around these two questions. So, what do we mean specifically by the term analytical culture? What does this mean for analytics and decision making?

Let's consider the Challenger example again. If the facts were acted upon, a tragic disaster could have been avoided. The question then arises: How do we design an organization and incentives so that it is only the facts that are acted upon? Blame is often assigned to the culture for all sorts of bad behavior and suboptimal results. Correct modeling, deep analytics, sophisticated algorithms, and statistical techniques are only part of the story. You also want to look at what specific behaviors are being rewarded and encouraged through incentives and who has the authority to make decisions.

2.2.5 *Optimal Incentive Contract for Collaboration: Sharing Control and Return Rights*

One of the most efficient incentive contracts is transferring the rights of ownership to nonowners. The two rights of ownership are *control rights* and *return rights*. Control rights are rights that come with ownership, which say that the owner has the right to do whatever he wants with the assets. Return rights are the rights to any returns, financial or otherwise, associated with the asset.

Sometimes the most efficient incentive contract is to transfer these rights of ownership to nonowners. In practice, this is done all the time. Executives are given a lot of freedom to make decisions about the assets of the organization, and they are in turn awarded some portion of the returns from the use of the assets. At the executive level, this sort of contract is generally a given. As we move to other positions in the organization, this might not be so common (ascribing both rights to employees).

There are many examples where one or the other of these rights is to some degree transferred to nonexecutive employees. There are many examples in which organizations provide opportunities for employees to participate in decisions or to manage assets that they are in direct contact with. The same applies to some degree of participation in the gains associated with the use of those assets. What is more unusual is for nonexecutives to have both of these rights transferred to them.

We need to explore three issues here:

- Transferring control rights without return rights does not provide an incentive to maximize the output from that asset (for example, either technological or human capital).

- Transferring the right of returns without transferring control rights means that employees will not have the authority to fully utilize the asset to obtain the maximum return. For example, they do not have the authority to cross-sell products.

- The most efficient incentive contract is when nonexecutives have both rights transferred to them. That is, they can cross-sell products and receive compensation for doing so.

2.2.6 Models of Collaboration

I have had the good fortune of being associated with two very collaborative and cooperative work environments. One was a research center at the London School of Economics (the Centre for Economic Performance; CEP). The other was the European headquarters of Cargill, Inc., located at that time in Cobham, Surrey.

They were both tremendously challenging and supportive cultures. They expected world-class cutting-edge social science research and world-class work, and no one in either place was shy about being as critical as they were supportive. Both of these places were filled with bright and hard-working individuals who valued competence and collaboration and a nice mix of work, play, and socializing. Strong ties developed between people, and people were happy to share their expertise with one another. I believe the cultures in these places were also the reason for their success. The CEP had two future Nobel Prize winners associated with it, and Cargill, Inc. is the largest private company in the world.

I have also worked where the environment was much more Darwinian—a place with little collaboration, where people routinely helped themselves to others ideas, took credit for others' work, and were generally (no other way to say it) mean spirited. I liked the collaborative places better.

Some people excel in Darwinian workplaces. Microsoft has this sort of reputation. Microsoft has enjoyed great success (being a near monopoly has not hurt), but I do not believe this model maximizes the potential benefits from individual and collective private information.

One organization that typifies many of the positive aspects of what I am advancing here is the SAS Institute, located in Cary, North Carolina. It also happens to be one of the premiere makers of advanced analytical software.

2.2.7 The SAS Institute

The SAS Institute was established in 1976 by five co-founders and is one of the top providers of analytical software in the world.[19] James Goodnight is the CEO and primary owner, controlling a two-thirds share of the company. SAS supplies many Fortune 500 companies with advanced analytical products.

Goodnight had worked for NASA, where employees were not trusted, executives were treated much differently from most workers, people did not talk to one another, and employee turnover was 50%. He vowed that if he were to start a company, things would be different; at SAS, they are.

Employees work a 35-hour workweek. There are on-site physicians, social workers, daycare, a gym—almost every service you can think of. The notion is that if daily tasks and concerns are taken care of, employees will be much more able to concentrate on their jobs.

One of the most impressive metrics is the fact that turnover is extremely low for a technology company. It hovers around 4%; the range for most technology companies is between 30% and 60%. It is estimated this low turnover rate saves the company $65 million annually, not including all the valuable information that employees take with them when they leave.

The organization is built upon a few important pillars, including the following:

- Invest heavily in getting the hire decision correct.
- Employees work a 35-hour workweek.
- No stock options, but profit sharing and bonuses.
- An annual employee and manager survey gauges morale.

SAS's compensation systems are designed to foster interdependence. For instance, individual targets are not set for salespeople; instead, sales team targets are established. How well they do as a team determines how well the salespeople are rewarded. If you hire the right people, this serves as a powerful incentive. It provides an incentive to both help each out and to monitor one another.

Also note that no stock options are given. Instead, everyone participates in a company profit-sharing scheme, and everyone is bonus eligible. I believe they are doing exactly the right thing by not offering stock options. SAS is a private company owned largely by Jim Goodnight, and though it is entirely possible for private firms to put in place a phantom stock-option program, in this case it is unnecessary and would detract from the type of organization in place.

And, it has to be said, they are a hugely successful organization. They make great products (I talk about a number of them), have always been profitable, have never laid anyone off, always issue profit-sharing payments, and continue to grow. They have an interesting business model where they lease software to companies, with a yearly renewal of the lease; so, they are extremely responsive to their customers. This model has been a pivotal component of their success.

2.2.8 EMC|One

An excellent example of an initiative with a focus on both the organizational culture and the technology was in place at EMC. During the recession, when there was a focus on cutting costs, many EMC employees used a social media platform to suggest ways to cut costs and increase efficiencies. Changes that were made were more palpable to employees because they were part of the decision-making process, and because of the aggregation of information from many, the decisions themselves were better.[20]

2.2.9 *Boston Scientific*

Another firm that does an especially good job with collaboration is Boston Scientific.[21] According to John Abele, one of its founders, one of the biggest challenges of developing a collaborative organization was not with the technology but rather with other factors. Abele emphasizes the importance of soft skills when it comes to something as critical as collaboration. Abele described a training course for a surgical method as follows:

> Its real value, though, lies in the "wisdom of crowds" approach to advancing and proliferating the best new techniques. Software tools for collaboration abound, but it's the soft skills that bring minds together.[22]

2.3 Advanced Analytics and Collaborative Decision Making

In the first instance, advanced analytics can assist with the determination of whether your organization, division, plant, department, or team could benefit from collaborative decision making. The decision framework should look like this:

1. Should you put in place a collaborative decision making process?

    A. Degree to which employees have access to potentially productivity enhancing information (1–10)

B. The impact that information could have on output (1–10)

C. Decision required immediately (1–10)

2. What form of collaborative decision-making process should you put into place?

2.3.1 Challenges and Opportunities with Participative Decision Making

Enterprise content management (ECM) software makes much of knowledge management and collaboration possible. These systems hold the text, videos, social media, and other content that ultimately facilitates the sharing of this information. Interestingly, while much of IT spending decreased during the recession, spending on ECM increased. Spending increased by 5.1% in 2009, and 7.6% in 2010 (with revenue for ECM in 2010 of $3.9 billion). Estimates suggest that the annual compound growth in ECM purchases will increase at 11.4% through 2015.[23]

This is not entirely difficult to explain. Firms were doing their best to do more with less, so employees were (apparently) using whatever information source they could find. Organizations purchase these systems for a number of reasons, including the following:[24]

- Improve effectiveness
- Reduce operational costs
- Optimize business processes
- Achieve regulatory compliance and e-discovery goals
- Attract and retain customers

A number of excellent tools can assist with the collaboration process and ultimately assist with the making of much better decisions. Organizations are also starting to get much better at this. Organizations that can tap into the knowledge skills and abilities of their workforces are at a sizable competitive advantage over those that do not.

Much of this is motivated by leveraging and retaining employee know-how. This is certainly the case in all knowledge-intensive firms such as consulting and research and in development-intensive industries. However, nearly all firms have institutional knowledge and experience that can be better leveraged.

You'll note in other chapters a partial focus on the use of analytics to *avoid* problems. In this section, most of the focus is on optimization. The underlying assumption here is that a treasure trove of information resides within employees, and because of all the technologies that have come online recently, it is critical to get the incentives and the organizational structure right.

In settings where there is little incentive to share information across divisions or even with fellow employees, intergroup cooperation is much more likely than intergroup competition to promote positive outcomes. Competition between groups is fine, but you increase your chance of success substantially if a strong element of cooperation exists within the organization.

2.3.2 *Software, Advanced Analytics, and Cooperation and Collaboration*

Business intelligence software has some functionality referred to as *collaborative BI*. However, these systems are not as comprehensive as collaborative decisions-making platforms.[25]

Here are some impressive software products that can assist with this process:

Cogniti

Decision Lens (CMD)

IBM Cognos BI V.10.1 (CMD and collaborative BI)

Lyasoft: Lyza (CDM and collaborative BI)

Microsoft SharePoint (CDM)

Panorama Software: Necto

Purus Technologies: DecisionSurface (CDM)

SAP: SAP StreamWork (CDM)

2.3.3 Deep Q&A Expert Systems

Where can decisions associated with collaboration and knowledge management be assisted by AI and deep Q&A expert systems? Quite a number of potential problems and opportunities can be addressed and opportunities uncovered. Cray Computer's YarcData has come out with a new computer called uRiKA (pronounced Eureka) that is similar to IBM's Watson:

- Determinant of the primary method of decision making in your organization

- Determinant of the optimal decision-making strategy for your organization

- Recommended course of action

As stated previously, many vendors are operating in this space, and there is not enough bandwidth in this book to profile them all. Again, excellent sources of information for comprehensive evaluation of the various vendors and their products include Gartner Research and Forrester Research. The specific vendors I discuss are so profiled because they provide features that I believe are especially pertinent to HCM decisions, with one caveat for this chapter. Generally, when discussing other software in this book, the discussion focuses on information associated with HCM and related decisions. This evaluation will not be limited to only HCM decisions but will instead include a broader set of decisions. These systems usually contain a variety of business intelligence, including a variety of decisions support tools. With regard to collaborative decision making (CDM) software, as with much of the software I discuss, the primary obstacle to use is organizational culture issues. Top management might not care to give up the power that comes with control over decision making. According to Gartner,[26] decisions associated with these systems include resource allocation, vendor selection, planning, and forecasting—all topics that are engaged with within HCM.

These systems facilitate the collaboration of many different parties to gather as much information as possible about an issue, ultimately using this information to suggest a more informed decision. Are the decisions better? This is a question that needs to be tested. Of course, with issues such as are they faster or slower, one would assume the decision making process may be slower, but this is not necessarily the case. Gathering all the information necessary to make a decision might seem to slow down the decision making, but making an informed decision certainly requires a substantial amount of research. This technology can speed up the process of obtaining the necessary information. So, the jury is out on this question of speed.

The quality of the decision is clearly a critically important aspect of the decision-making process. What about evidence that decisions using analytics are more robust? Again, there is a clear impact on performance associated with the use of advanced analytics. One such CDM system is the SAP StreamWork. The system is stand alone and allows whomever is the decision maker to find and select the best possible people to be included in the decision-making process based on information found in their profile. It provides signoff capability for those with various degrees of authority. It also captures the entire decision-making process and documents and stores it so that it can be revisited. The system interfaces with other SAP systems, making it possible to upload spreadsheets and dashboards, polls, pro/con tables, and a number of decision-making tools. In addition, it is possible to collaborate with external customers and clients, at the same time that confidential worksheets are kept confidential.

So, this in turn boils down to a simple question: What specifically can we do to see that our information capital is maximized? And how can advanced analytics assist with this process? If you want to be convinced that we do an especially lousy job with prediction, look no further than merger and acquisitions. We are truly terrible at predicting which firms are likely to work well in concert. Much of this boils down to incomplete and inaccurate predictive models.

3

Value Creation and Advanced Analytics

3.1 The Wealth of Organizations and What Advanced Analytics Can Do

If there are tectonic changes associated with our understanding of how we make decisions and what actually comprises human nature, the same holds true for our understanding of where value lies within organizations. Historically, financial and technological capital was considered the primary driver of value creation.[1] More recently, they have come to be viewed as commodities—essential inputs, but easily transferable and (generally) readily available. (If you are working for a cash-strapped start-up, small company, or in a dying industry, *readily* available financial capital might not ring true. However, if you are associated with any of the Fortune 500 with its $2 trillion in cash reserves, it may.) It is also increasingly understood that the input that does not lend itself easily to commoditization is inputs from human capital.

The reason human capital is so difficult to commoditize is because it possess something other forms of capital do not: *asymmetric* or private information. Unlike financial or technical capital, if it so chooses human capital can keep what it knows to itself, withhold effort, or, frankly, just leave. To maximize the contribution of human capital, employers develop incentive contracts—policies and practices developed to enable and motivate the workforce. When these practices and policies that maximize human capital's contribution are combined with other complementary forms of organizational capabilities (for example, work processes, technologies), it becomes nearly impossible for the competition to replicate, consequently providing a powerful and sustainable competitive advantage. The trick is to determine exactly which policies and practices for your *specific human capital and organizational capabilities* optimally promote your organizational objectives.

Getting human capital management (HCM) policies and practices right provides two main benefits. One, you will be much more likely to retain the human capital that is associated with your success, and two, you will have greater output, more innovative products and services, much more satisfied customers, and greater product and service quality. Consequently, this will result in cost savings (employee turnover is very expensive) and greater growth.

The use of advanced analytics can assist in making these determinations much more accurately. You can do this in a number of specific ways, including the following:

- *Predict* much more accurate outcomes.
  - Use better models of organizational value creation.
  - Model how humans actually decide.
  - Utilize agent-based modeling.
- *Recommend* optimal practice and policy choice.
  - Determine optimal policy and practice.
  - Deep Q&A expert systems.
- *Signal* more accurately ability and potential.
  - Determine optimal selection and promotion.
  - Use bibliographical data.

- *Map* individual and team performance to organizational outcomes.
  - Performance management and incentives.
  - Map contribution to organizational objectives.
- *Share* knowledge and know-how.
- *Evaluate* the impact of planned and potential policy and practice changes.
- *Optimize* employment levels, hours worked, and benefits.
- *Diagnose* problems and recommend solutions.

3.1.1 Information Capital

As discussed in Chapter 2, "Collaboration, Cooperation, and Reciprocity," human capital has private or asymmetric information, information that only they know. This information can relate to skills and abilities or how hard they can really work or information about customers, new products, or ways to make the production process more efficient and effective. This information that only they know has considerable value, a quantifiable value.

The existence of asymmetric information is the reason why the effective management of human capital is so critical for organizational success. This is also one of the primary reasons why it is critically important to retain key human capital. One of the primary reasons employee turnover is so costly is because employees have a bad habit of taking what they know with them when they leave. Human capital has the unique ability to decide what information it cares to share and what information to keep to itself. However, there is another source of information that also has tremendous value to organizations, and that information is found in data, the data organizations keep on their human capital.

3.1.2 *Constant and Unrelenting Experimentation*

Every organization is unique, and so is everyone working within it. That in itself provides a strong argument that the notions of best practice (it should work for everyone everywhere) and benchmarking (comparing base salaries, for instance) should become less and less important. This does not mean that seeing what the "market" is up to is not valuable, but in terms of really achieving an impossible-to-replicate competitive advantage, you want to *know what works for you.* What this requires, and what we have the tools to achieve, is constant and unrelenting experimentation.

Most organizations have everything they need to constantly be evaluating and, more important, experimenting with new ideas and ways to engage, enable, and excite the human capital. This does not mean that you have to roll out a tremendously expensive new program, but you can experiment at one work site or with a work team and see how the new initiative is received. We should always have the answer to this question: Is the program worth it? Or, did the program work? For instance, one type of program that has been around for a long time is the organizational wellness program. Do these programs save the organization money or not?[2]

Take, for example, Yahoo!'s new policy that requires everyone to come into the office. There is an identifiable date, so assuming that they have the necessary data, they have everything they need to determine whether (after the introduction of that new policy) employee turnover decreased, increased, or stayed the same. They can look at absenteeism, employee morale, whether the company developed more innovative products, the number of customer complaints, and so on, ultimately determining if there is a relationship between the introduction of this new policy and outcomes of interest.

Panel data analysis provides us with the means to determine the holy grail of econometric analysis. This type of analysis allows us to evaluate (and hopefully establish) a cause and effect relationship, enabling us ultimately to say declaratively that a particular policy and practice was closely associated with a specific outcome. Time series or panel analysis consists of evaluating the impact the introduction a policy and practice has on variables of interest. For example, you just put in place a child-care facility in your office in New York, but not in California. Once some time passes, say three months, you have pretty much everything you need to conduct impactful econometric analysis, establishing (or not) a cause and effect relationship between the use of a specific practice and the impact on outcomes of interests. Those outcomes can include everything from employee turnover, absentee-ism, sales, and customer satisfaction, to name a few.

Organizations are constantly conducting cost benefit analysis associated with market plans, new products, and so forth. However, the same sort of analysis associated with costing HCM issues is done less often. Organizations can experiment in different ways to evaluate and refine policies and practices that are in place and thus tailor their activities to obtain the maximum long-term positive impact.

3.1.3 Gold in Them There Databases: Human Capital Data

One of the projects I worked on while I was working at the Center for Economic Performance (CEP) at the London School of Economics was a Data for Analysis exchange. The arrangement was if organizations would provide researchers at the CEP with data from their human resources information system (HRIS), we would use that data for publications, and in turn we would provide them with a rigorous and thorough evaluation of the impact of the policies and practices they had in place. At the time in Britain, the late 1990s, there was con-siderable speculation that a minimum wage was going to go into effect, and it did in 1999. Researchers were interested in the impact this would have on employment. The standard economic argument holds that as wages increase, we buy less, in this case employees; so based on this theory, we should see unemployment go up. Here again there is at best mixed evidence supporting conventional economic theory. Yes, if the minimum wage is very high, organizations are less likely to hire. However, there is an optimal pay level in which employee turnover drops (these are most likely service sector jobs) and profits increase (again, it is not rocket science: having to constantly hire and train people is costly). I considered this data bartering/analysis arrangement to be a marriage made in heaven, a top research university providing an organization with rigorous, unbiased, and objective research, and the CEP would get some really great data. The organizations could remain anonymous if they so chose, and they would get for free an analysis that would normally cost them a lot of money.

One frustration I had when working for organizations was that we never really had time to evaluate the impact of the practices we were putting in place. We were so tied up with the immediate day-to-day activities that evaluating the effectiveness of what we were doing was not on the radar. At the time, I knew that was suboptimal, because conducting this sort of analysis could provide extremely valuable information on the impact of the policies and practices in place, and also inform future decisions about what to do. We (I was really just involved in the project at the very beginning) did end up getting a number of organizations to participate, and those that did participate got some really great analysis, and scholars at the CEP were able to publish some great papers using the data.

When people think about valuable data, they often think about data on consumer spending habits or people's search results, which is information that is ultimately very valuable to advertising organizations. Less often considered is the treasure trove of data organizations have on their own primary driver of organizational success: human capital.

Organizations usually have a large amount of data on employee salary histories and demographic data. There is also data on training and performance appraisals and possibly employee satisfaction surveys. In addition, and very importantly, there is data on the date a new incentive plan was put into place (for example, when the child-care facility started or when a wellness program was established). Couple this with organizational performance data and you are able conduct a panel data analysis that provides a clear cause and effect relationship. Often, unfortunately, at best data is used to show correlations between two variables. Yes, information from correlations may point us in the right direct (or the wrong one), but it says nothing about cause and effect. Here again is an opportunity provided to us by big HCM data and sophisticated analytics. (I have not talked about how critical data integrity is, but it is a fundamental starting point.) We can use this information to both evaluate what we have done and to make better decisions about what to do in the future.

3.1.4 Not Only Human Experts Are Prone to Biases

As discussed earlier, relying on the experience of one human expert exposes decisions to biases but the same can be said when evaluating empirical research. Empirical research is subject to different but no less problematic biases including the following:

- **Measurement error:** Are you accurately measuring the concept you are attempting to measure (for example, employee morale and satisfaction)?

- **Omitted variable bias:** Is the observed result influenced by factors not included in your model (for example, variation in the quality of managers)?

- **Reverse causality:** Do higher profits make happier employees or do happier employees make higher profits?

3.2 Value and How to Create It: Intangible Capital

In addition to paradigm-shifting discoveries about how we make decisions and how rational we really are, there has been paradigm-shifting research related to what makes organizations successful and the role human capital plays in this process. Much of this research has been conducted by Baruch Lev of NYU's Stern School of Management[3] and his students. Intangible capital is defined as all those factors that ultimately lead to value creation, including reputation, intellectual property, and human capital.

Increasingly, the question is being asked: What drives intangible capital formation? While a substantial amount of the discussion has revolved around the issue of the measurement of intangibles,[4] the work of those like Robert Kaplan and David Norton has gone a long way toward identifying how it is formed and developed. One of the key drivers of intangible assets is inputs from human capital.

3.2.1 Who Really Holds the Keys to the Kingdom

A term used to describea combination of IT, human capital, and other organizational capabilities is *organizational capital*.

One definition of organizational capital is:[5]

The knowledge used to combine human skills and physical capital into systems for producing and delivering want-satisfying products. It relates but is not limited to the following: (a) operating capabilities; (b) investment capabilities; and (c) innovation capabilities.[6]

Others view organizational capital as primarily residing within human capital,[7] and still others view it as embodied in the organization itself.[8] Organizational capital recognizes that inputs from human capital combined with other organizational capabilities are the primary value creation mechanisms within organizations.

Yu Peng Lin and I were interested in just what role organizational capital played as a mechanism for why we were seeing better performance in companies that broadly distributed stock options. As mentioned, organizational capital is meant to identify organizational capabilities, human and technological. By evaluating a measure of organizational capital, we were able to determine whether the higher degree of output was due to this combination of human and technical capital. We found strong evidence that stock options were associated with greater organizational capital and greater output.[9]

This research showed that much of the value created from stock options was due to an increase in organizational capital, and we concluded that this was also associated with much lower employee turnover. This finding, along with substantial other research, points us toward making certain that employee turnover is kept as low as possible. This, in turn, means that the value-creating mechanism within an organization is largely a function of inputs from human capital. This is not to suggest that the other inputs are not necessary, but maximizing the contribution of human capital is the way to create significant value in the organization.

It is difficult to adequately emphasize just how critical it is, for the well-being of the organization, to keep key employee turnover as low as possible. When an organization finds someone who is an especially good fit, the organization should ensure that they are motivated, satisfied, and challenged. Due to its vesting requirement, broad-based stock options are especially good at keeping employees tied to the organization. This "retention effect" ultimately results in greater output and financial returns.

Again, I want to emphasize that this does not mean that every organization everywhere would be better off if they offered stock options to everyone. The key is to have an engaged workforce, and there are many ways in which to accomplish this, depending on the nature of the organization and the workforce.

3.2.2 *The Nature of the Organization*

Although it might sound esoteric and philosophical, the topic of the nature of the organization has very practical implications. Why firms or organizations exist at all is a question that has engaged the social sciences for a very long time. Within economics, the answer to this question is largely found within the "transaction cost" literature. This literature states that it is much more efficient to conduct certain activities under the umbrella of an organization. What is important to rememberis that all organizations at their most elemental are simply coordination and incentive systems. So, this boils down to two simple questions:

- Who does what?
- How do we get them to do it?

3.2.3 *The Cost of Employee Turnover*

The direct costs associated with employee turnover has been estimated to be anywhere from 1.5× annual salary to as high at 5× for difficult-to-fill positions. So, the direct (executive search fees, time spent recruiting and interviewing, and so on) is in and of itself substantial. These are all easily identified costs that should be fairly easy to extract if you want to determine an exact cost for your organization. However, these costs are really just a small part of the overall cost to an organization when employees with valuable information leave the organization.

You are also losing all their accumulated organizational-specific human capital. We will see that keeping employee turnover as low as possible makes especially good sense if you have employees who have access to very valuable information in the form of information on customers, new products or services, product quality, and their own human capital; and this means just about everyone.

Keeping employee turnover as low as possible justifies investing in programs and policies that are focused specifically on that end. For instance, child-care services, or a health club, or deferred compensation, whatever policies fit your specific organization. As mentioned, the company SAS has onsite health care, child care, and social workers available to assist with elder care and other family issues. These programs all allow employees to focus on their jobs, and they also serve to keep employee turnover low. The related costs of these programs are more than paid for by the 4% or 5% annual employee turnover that this company sees versus the 20% or higher rate in the rest of their industry.

3.3 Strategic Choice and Advanced Analytics

At the time I worked for Cargill, Inc., the company employed both distressed asset traders and cowboys. Do you think the same policy and practices should be in place for both types of employee? Do you think the same policies and practices should treat both job families the same? Do you think what motivates a cowboy is the same as what motivates a financial trader? What makes for a great cowboy? What makes for a great distressed asset trader? Probably not the same characteristics.

Oddly, many organizations and some of the research has long looked for *best practices*. These are practices and policies that work every time for everyone; essentially, one size fits all. Does following the best practice philosophy actually optimize the contribution from human capital? The answer is no. What motivates a cowboy will not motivate a derivative trader, and, for that matter, what motivates one cowboy will differ significantly from what motivates another.

The stock option example I mention in the first chapter is another example. Yes, broadly dispersed stock options are associated with greater levels of productivity, but the important qualifier is that this in no way means that everyone should give options to everyone or to anyone for that matter. Nor does it even mean that every technology firm should use stock options. The company I mentioned earlier, SAS, a tremendously successful privately owned company (giving phantom options in private firms is done often) does not give anyone stock options. They have one of the lowest turnover rates in the industry. The practices and policies you put in place depend entirely on what you are trying to accomplish and with whom.

Effective human capital management has been defined as follows:

A pattern of planned human resource deployments and activities intended to enable an organization to achieve its goals.[10]

An issue that needs immediate attention in a world of practically an unlimited number of potential HCM deployments and activities is this: Which specific ones are the most effective in any particular situation? Recently, there has been some controversy surrounding the optimal choice of policy and practices.

There are two aspects to strategic HR issues: first, the *determination* of the optimal way in which the HR policies and practices can support the objectives of the firm; and second, the *execution* of these policies and practices. The use of advanced analytics and emerging technologies can assist considerably with the determination of optimal HR policy and practice choice, and the emerging technologies can go a long way toward the execution of the various policies and practices.

This is the domain of strategic HR management, and ideally, to make optimal choices, you want to consider a combination of micro and macro factors. What practices make the ideal choice under specific situations, and how can advanced analytics assist with that?

An equation for this model is as follows:

Organizational Strategy + HR Policies and Practices = Organizational Success

3.3.1 HCM Practice Choice and Advanced Analytics

According to Bruce Kaufman and Ben Miller, authors of the article "The Firm's Choice of HRM Practices: Economics Meets Strategic Human Resource Management," the primary question associated with strategic human resource management research (SHRM) is this: "What is the firm's optimal (performance maximizing) choice of HRM practices?"[11] The authors review a number of different approaches associated with HR practice determination, including the following:[12]

- **Universalistic:** The universalistic approach holds that there are certain best practices that should be adopted by everyone everywhere because they will universally promote superior performance. The specific practice choice in the universalistic approach is not well defined, and this approach consists largely of general concepts (for example, extensive training, decentralized decision making, extensive information sharing).

- **Contingency:** The contingency approach holds that the choice of practice is contingent on the specific situation. This view adopts a best fit approach contingent on factors such as firm size, skill level and tasks of the workforce, labor market conditions, and so on.

- **Configurational:** The configurational approach consists of a systems approach in which the various HR functions (for example, recruitment, selection, training, compensation) complement one another.

Assumed within these approaches is that the potential performance effect is multiplicative; that is, the more of them you use, the greater the impact on performance. There seems to be general agreement that the "one size fits all" approach is faulty and so, instead, an integrated approach is the most sensible approach.

Consequently, how do we model ideal HR practice choice? According to Kaufman and Miller, management scholars generally consider economic models to be too simplistic,[13] and economists view management as light on substance and heavy on description and prescription.[14] However, the authors draw from both the management and economic traditions to determine the factors to consider when deciding what practices to put in place that are most closely associated with successful outcomes. More recently, there has been a focus on what has been referred to a "high performance work practices" (HPWP) or practices that engage and motive the workforce. However, it is also recognized that these practices vary by situation.

This model is well suited for explaining (or in our case determining) practice choice across industry, organizational life cycle, firm size, country, and so on and predicts the use of the various practices within a particular setting. The Xi variable is the one of interest to us. This variable is actually a vector (or list) of practices associated with optimal HCM practice choice.

- **Firm size:** The demand should increase with the size of the organization.
- **Wages:** If you are paying above market rate, expending effort on maximizing the contribution of human capital is very important.
- **Technology:** Team production.

In essence, the model uses the following equation when attempting to determine optimal choice:

$$HRMi=f(Qi,Wi,Xi)$$

The next question is this: What practice do we use when? The answer to this question will vary considerably depending on the situation you are in. In many cases, the default has been to put in place the same HR policies and practices that a competitor (or an organization that is operating in the same labor market, which may or may not be in the same industry) uses. Because there are few true apples-to-apples situations, it is most efficient to take the time to carefully evaluate your individual situation. This is not to say that knowing a competitor's policies and practices is not valuable, but the adoption of exactly what they are doing is rarely advisable.

Suppose, for instance, that you are about to open a new plant in a different part of the country, or maybe in another country. You have some data on local pay rates and the kind of practices that the competitors have in place. However, it is a green field site in a business your organization is new to. How do you decide what policies and practices to put into place? You need to abide by existing laws and the other conventions of the region or country, but you still have plenty of latitude to choose policies and practices that you believe will maximize organizational efficiency.

The information necessary to make policy and practice determination is easily handled by tools associated with advanced analytics, but not so easily handled by us. The choice of policy and practices and how they align with the other HR policies and practices can quickly become complicated. This is due to the large number of different HR policies and practices that exist. You have to consider which ones maximize the potential for meeting organizational objectives as well as how they interact with all the other organizational and functional policies and practices in place.

3.3.2 Business Intelligence Alignment of HCM Practices and Policies with Business Strategy

There have been a number of developments in business intelligence (BI) and analytics recently. These developments involve the use of ever-more sophisticated analytics and the presentation of those analytics. In addition, there have been advances within the HR profession, providing much clearer insights into how and where effective decisions are made.

The use of analytics has a long history within HR as well, with many practitioners and academics alike making formidable contributions to the discipline. Much of this work has concentrated on the use of analytics to establish a connection between HR activities and the performance of the firm.

Increasingly, strategy maps are being used for more robust analysis. This is important because to date many of the analytics available only allowed for simple descriptive analytics. More recently developed analytical tools enable you to be much more declarative about whether two variables have a causal relationship. For example, these systems should allow an answer to questions such as this: Has the introduction of a new on-site child-care facility resulted in an increase in employee morale and a decrease in employee turnover? Then, ideally, it would be of further benefit to determine the exact dollar impact the adoption of a child care facility. Are the costs associated with setting up and running an on-site child-care facility more or less than the cost savings associated with reducing employee turnover and absenteeism? Also, are there added benefits associated with the establishment of the on-site child-care facility? For instance, is there a benefit associated with the attraction of potential new employees?

3.3.3 Decision Science, Business Intelligence, and Implications for HCM Decisions

It is generally agreed that the field of decision science got its start with Fredrick Taylor in the early 1900s.[15] Fredrick Taylor is, of course, known for *scientific management* and *Taylorism* and his use of time-motion studies to determine optimal job rates, which was in turn tied to pay and the infamous "piece rate" systems that rewarded quantity over quality. Taylor may have gotten things started, but decision science[16] did not really take off until WWII, during which the techniques were applied to strategic and tactical problems during the war. Simultaneously, an increase in computing power allowed for more and more sophisticated analysis.

The challenge with decision science is the emphasis has long been on how people *should* make decisions rather than on how people actually do make decisions. Fast forward to today and sophisticated BI analytics are mostly found within finance and general strategy products. They include such products as IBM's CFO Performance Dashboard version 3 Advanced Edition and SAS' Strategy Management.[17] One big advantage of these systems is that they allow for rigorous evaluation of the relationships between variables. IBM's CFO Performance Dashboard,[18] for instance, provides financial key performance indicators (KPIs), and it integrates IBM's Cognos BI software and IBM's SPSS statistical capabilities. This provides a financial intelligence and allows for "what if" analysis and also includes predictive analysis using causal modeling that provides potential outcomes associated with specific business decisions and scenarios.

Although considerable variation exists across industries, on average 70% of the cost of doing business is due to human capital costs. Consequently, the more this resource is optimized, the better; and advanced analytics provides a number of tools that can assist with this. Advanced analytics offers a number of potential ways in which to make better decisions about HR policy and practice choice, including the following:

- Dashboards, scorecards, and strategy maps can be used to better understand relationships between variables and assist in establishing line-of-sight causal relationships between performance outcomes.

- Advanced analytics with predictive capabilities can establish connections between programs and policies and organizational performance outcomes (for example, productivity, profitability, employee turnover, employee morale).

• Q&A expert systems can assist with the determination of optimal HR policy and practice choice.

• Applications can help diagnose problematic outcomes such as employee turnover.

Recent work has established a connection between effective HR management and firm performance.[19]

The alignment of HCM practices with business objectives has evolved into how these policies and practices map to organizational objectives. Many of the corporate performance management strategy products display the relationships between various metrics and how they co-vary. This largely takes place though the use of dashboards, scorecards, enterprise metrics frameworks, and the analysis of structured and unstructured data.[20] According to Forrester Research, a number of BI vendors offer "consolidated HR analytics solutions."[21] The benefit of these sorts of products is that they allow integration across a variety of different enterprise resource planning (ERP) vendors.

3.3.4 Machine Learning and HR Practice Choice

What can machine learning add to the determination and execution of the selection and execution of HR policies and practices? Once the initial model is established, the next stage can be to further determine whether there are other patterns associated with policy choice and practices and stated objectives. As discussed, machine learning is especially good at pattern identification. HR is a data-intensive function. Machines that learn can do just that and can comb through a wide range of data looking for patterns.

- **Machine learning**

  Identify why turnover is taking place.

  "Learn" what characteristics are associated with superior performance.

- **Predictive modeling**

  Use machine learning to better predict whom you will need to hire in the future.

- **Deep Q&A expert systems**

  Get advice based on rigorous research rather than one person's opinion.

- **Prescriptive recommendations**

  What can deep Q&A systems assist us with relative to determination of policy practice and choice?

Again, the policies and practices in place are often a function of tradition or benchmarking. What may have made sense 10 years ago or relative to the plant next to you in a totally different industry and in a different point in the life cycle will almost certainly not be pertinent to your given situation.

3.4 Software Applications, Analytics, and HR Decisions

Interesting technologies that have considerable potential for impacting HCM decision making are strategy maps and sophisticated scorecards that include analytics and that are integrated within an ERP system. These can provide a very rich set of information and data that allows for forecasting and what-if analysis and that can go a long way toward establishing a cause and effect relationship between practice choice and outcomes.

Most people doing HCM are too busy with the transactional to have time to engage in analysis. The potential of these systems is substantial. For instance, it is possible to start with an inventory of employee skills to match those with the strategic objectives of the firm. This is what these systems now allow for. Much of the advanced analytics consist of the following three capabilities:

- **Forecasting capabilities** are used to accurately assess future needed skills. It is also possible to evaluate the needed skills mix using a variety of different scenarios. An example is the potential entrance into new markets requiring a new set of capabilities.

- **Predictive modeling** allows for an analysis of past events to predict future outcomes and assess both areas of opportunity and risk. For instance, it is possible to identify employees who are at high risk of leaving the organization, allowing time to develop interventions to reduce undesirable turnover.

- **Optimization** provides a method to determine the ideal allocation of resources (for example, allocation of a bonus pool across employees while keeping an eye on internal and external equity).

3.4.1 *Software Options and Optimal HCM Practice*

This would often be associated with the notion of strategic HCM. Alignment of HR practices with business objectives is critical to organizational success. Much of this boils down to an interface of human capital, with technological capital (e.g., I.T. systems).

A number of specific tools do an outstanding job of helping to make decisions that ultimately impact the success of the organization. One of the most integrated systems is SuccessFactor'sBizX, short for Business Execution Software.

The software offers a complete set of applications, including the following:

- **Performance and Goals:** Facilitates the communication of individual goals and enables managers and executives to monitor how individuals are progressing on goals and to issue rewards when objectives are met.

- **Compensation:** Ties performance appraisals and performance management to rewards.

- **Recruitment:** This application provides a means to track and manage perspective candidates and also provides access to social media and a means of collaborating within the organization to facilitate decision making.

- **Learning:** Mostly an e-learning or a learning as management solution (LMS).

- **Collaboration:** This refers to a mobile collaborative device providing a mechanism to assist with decision making and information sharing.

- **Workforce Planning:** Allows for forecasting the impact of a variety of strategies.

- **Employee Central:** A user-friendly HR self-service data center.

- **Workforce Analytics and Reporting:** Provides actionable intelligence to decision makers.

3.4.2 Enterprise Resource Planning Software

One of the competitive advantages (perhaps the primary advantage) of ERP software is its integration with all the other systems, such as finance, marketing, operations, and IT. Because HR is a part of a larger whole and always needs to support business objectives, ERP software is a nice fit.

A number of significant factors are currently impacting ERP software systems.[22] One factor is that more and more organizations are moving from an on-premise application of cloud-based software as service (SaaS) or platform as a service (PaaS) model. There is also a movement toward including a broader range of functionalities. Stand-alone applications such as applicant tracking systems are now integrated in with e-recruitment software, which are further integrated with workplace planning software, compensation, corporate leaning, collaboration systems, and so on. These combinations are called *talent management suites* and offer the advantage of integration of information. Finally, there will be further development of mobile apps and interaction with external data (for example, with social media).

That may well be the mission of Amazon when their data analytics recommend a book that we would never have chosen on our own but end up loving. This sort of computation logic allows for not only utilization of historical time series analysis but is now able to further interact with real-time data as well.[23]

3.4.3 *Talent Analytics*

IBM's Cognos Workforce Talent Analytics provides a broad suite of packaged reports and tools, including the following:

- **Talent Acquisition:** Their system provides an analysis of costs and the time it will take to acquire talent. It also analyzes the current pool of talent and how accurate its source is (for example, executive search firm).
- **Succession Planning:** Tracks current employees to identify and fill vacant positions.
- **Talent Retention:** Tracks the retention of employees.
- **Talent Development:** Measures costs and effectiveness of training programs on the skills and development of employees and how well they meet organizational goals.

3.4.4 SAS Business Intelligence

The SAS Human Capital Management software (version 5.2.1, as of this writing) provides comprehensive HCM advanced analytics that help with all the primary analytical functions, including forecasting, prediction, optimization, and scenario planning. Overall, this software provides a method to align the firm with organizational objectives.

SAS HCM software includes a number of useful tools that enable forecasting, predictive modeling, and optimization. One feature allows for the identification of top-performing employees who are at risk of leaving. In addition, SAS offer both time series and structural equation modeling. This provides significant help with establishing cause and effect between variables. Other advantages include the following:

- The system provides prepackaged metrics that provide a view of metrics such as revenue per employee and how close it is to established goals.

- Allows for "what if" analysis, providing a means of better anticipating a variety of workforce planning scenarios.

- Integrated in with the other SAS solutions and so can be used to see where the organization is relative to goals.

3.4.5 Talent Scorecard

SAS's Talent Scorecard is essentially a strategy map for HCM that enables the following:[24]

- Establishment of a link between strategy and execution. It does this by tracking KPIs.

- Establishment of cause and effect relationships (one of its biggest benefits). This is possible through evaluating variation between KPIs and goals.

- Alignment. One key benefit of these systems is that you can customize the metrics to your situation and thus allow for alignment of practices with strategy.

- Determination of potential challenges and opportunities through the use of alerts.

3.4.5.1 Human Capital Budgeting/Planning

This is one of the more interesting and exciting SAS solutions. It integrates SAS Human Capital Management with SAS Financial Management. This provides a link between operational strategy, human capital strategy, and financial strategy. It goes further and allows for predictive analytics and what-if analysis.

3.4.5.2 Predictive Workforce Analytics

It uses predictive modeling to identify employees at high risk of leaving. It further provides analysis of how skills shortages may impact the larger organization. It provides a mechanism for determining who might leave and who may stay. Again, it is used primarily for forecasting, descriptive and predictive modeling, and optimization.

3.4.5.3 Strategy Maps and Advanced Analytics

Many of the strategy map applications mirror the rationale associated with Robert Kaplan and David Norton's balanced scorecard. The overall approach is an attempt to better understand the links between execution and results. Essentially, they operationalize the theory of intangible capital.[25]

According to Kaplan and Norton:

Executives in all sectors and in all parts of the world were facing the dual challenges of how to mobilize their human capital and information resources.[26]

3.4.6 Talent Management Suites and Advanced Analytics

Gartner began reporting on talent management suites in 2005, and in 2011, they started to evaluate them as a single market.[27] One advantage associated with these suites is that they enable vertical and horizontal integration between a company's various functional areas and the various functional areas associated with HCM.

According to Gartner, a large portion of these systems were used for reporting. More recently, as I have already discussed, scorecards and dashboards have been added. However, these too can often be used primarily in a descriptive manner, rather than for predictive purposes.

Integrated systems such as these offer a number of advantages. There are advantages associated with having all the information in one place, and, of course, there are cost efficiencies associated with such integrated systems.

Increasingly, HCM software has consolidated. So, what were once independent functions are now all included in one suite.[28] These suites include some or all of the following functions:

- Workforce planning
- Talent acquisition
- Compensation
- Performance management
- Career development
- Succession planning
- Corporate learning

In addition, the inclusion of the following functions would prove valuable:

- Integration with broader ERP (for example, finance and operations)
- Social networking
- Collaborative decision-making software

4

Human Science and Selection Decisions

4.1 Optimizing Selection and Promotion Decisions

One of the few criticism of Sheryl Sandberg's (with Nell Scovell) book *Lean In* is that it focuses mostly on the supply side (what women should be doing) rather than the demand side (what organizations can do to eliminate biases).[1] During my own review of the topic of biases in selection and promotion decisions, I found substantial room for improvement needed at the organizational and institutional level. The extent of gender bias alone in our organizations remains formidable. According to findings by the Organization for Economic Co-operation and Development (OECD), in member countries, women are 17% less likely to be employed and earn 20% less than men.[2]

Why this matters is because any hiring or promotion decision based on factors other than who is the best candidate for the job will ultimately lead to suboptimal performance outcomes. What can advanced analytics do to assist with eliminating biases? A lot. Biased decision making is discrimination, and using advanced analytics to assist in the decision-making process will help eliminate biases. What difference does eliminating bias make? Also, a lot. Getting the right person in the right job drastically improves the probability of success.

I, however, have a bias (although it is not actually a bias because that suggests it is unfounded) when it comes to selection decisions.

Time spent making as robust a decision as possible is time very well spent. It is in everyone's self-interest to be working in a meritocracy (in effect, where people are doing what they are best suited to be doing). In this type of organization, it is not the loudest, the prettiest, or the boss's nephew who gets the job or the promotion. Instead, it is the person most likely to perform in the position. Any and all extraneous factors are eliminated from the selection decision, including the obvious demographic qualities (age, race, gender, disability, and so on). Also eliminated are factors like school attended, how well the interview went, how good someone's golf game is, and various other factors that decision makers may have a bias about but that have no bearing on job performance.

4.1.1 Performance and Selection

I do my grocery shopping at a large chain store close to where I live. I go there pretty much daily to pick up my lunch and any other food I need. One of my pet peeves is disengaged or generally uninterested check-out people—especially those who toss my food items in the bag without paying any attention to product crushability. Generally, they are quite good. On occasion, though, I arrive home to find the raspberries and nectarines crushed beneath the peanut butter. So, recently, when I was there picking up some things, I could not help but notice the extreme care with which the check-out person was taking when packing my purchases. He packed, unpacked, arranged, and rearranged my items and was especially careful with products high on the crushability index. I complimented him on the fine job he was doing, and we discussed the variation found in the performance of check-out people. I asked him about the training he received (a couple of hours) and asked whether everyone received the same training (they did) and if there was a mechanism in place to financially reward those like him who did such a fine job (there was not). I went on to say that it is a little odd that it is not customary to "tip" check-out folks—because like waitresses and waiters, the customer is in direct contact and the quality of the service provided matters (to me and my nectarines anyway). He really liked the idea (or at least that someone would suggest it). Finally, I asked directly what motivated him to do such an excellent job, to which he replied, "I simply pack other peoples food like I would pack my own."

This chain would be very wise to do everything in its power to retain and motivate this individual and, frankly, clone him. Much of what this chapter covers suggests how the use of tools from advanced analytics could allow this chain to do the next best thing to replicating him.

4.1.2 Making the Unobservable Observable

One big advantage of using data analytics is that it can assist with making what is unobservable observable. As discussed earlier, the notion of asymmetric information recognizes that only the individual really knows how hard he or she can work and his or her own ability. Organizations spend a large amount of time identifying proxies to assess ability and predict potential contribution (for example, GPA and college major). An example is the job interview, which has not been shown to be a very good predictor of job success.

You may have wondered how people like Bill Gates, Steve Jobs, Larry Ellison, or Mark Zuckerberg (or David Karp, founder of Tumblr and who did not finish high school) could be so successful without finishing college. (Alternatively, you might wonder how so many who graduated from college *are* successful.) According to economic theory, one advantage to getting an education is that it sends a signal, a signal that someone is high ability. It signals that they can stick with something to its completion and have the ability necessary to see that it is accomplished. As we become better at identifying attributes associated with success, increasingly, these traditional signals have less meaning. Each of the company founders listed has great vision and ability, and many of the normal signals (educational certification, GPA) were just not necessary.

The fact is, if you have the ability and the skills and have acquired the necessary knowledge, the formal degree and all the traditional check lists are becoming less important. This does not mean that I am disparaging a college education. For me, college was transformational; new worlds (countries anyway) were opened up to me. The point is that the better we get at measuring ability, aptitude, and potential, proxies become less relevant.

4.1.3 Eliminating Biases from Selection Decisions

SAP recently announced its plans to staff 1% of its workforce with people on the autism spectrum by 2020. They have found that having employees with autism increases productivity and engagement.

In 2009, Gary Moore and Dan Selic established the nonPareil Institute.[3] The charter of the institute is to provide those on the autism spectrum with training and technical job skills. This spectrum includes those at the high-functioning end who may have Asperger syndrome. This syndrome is characterized by difficulty with social interaction but also being very logical and very focused (traits important for computer programmers).

Some computer programmer will tell you that communication skills are very important when it comes to being a successful programmer. For some coding projects, this is certainly true. Others will tell you that it depends on the type of programming that you are doing. For example, if you are managing projects and coding, then social skills are critical. However, if your job mostly focuses on the actual coding associated with the project, and even if the project requires interaction between programmers, as long as the communication is focused on the task, those on the autism spectrum may perform exceptionally.

We all have our preconceived notions of what autism is, and so we might consciously or unconsciously exclude those with autism from consideration for a lot of things, including jobs. If we were to instead focus on the specific job, and the characteristics that makes for an excellent programmer *in a specific setting,* someone on the autistic spectrum could (and has been shown to) make a superb employee.

This is what advanced analytical tools enable us to do. We can use them to establish ever-closer approximation of fit between the task or job and those who function in those jobs. This is what advanced analytical tools enable us to do. We can use them to establish ever-closer approximations of fit between the task or job and those who function in those jobs.

4.1.4 Human Science and Employee Selection

Advanced analytics has gained substantial traction in employee selection. Numerous companies have come up with innovative ways to predict who will make the best employees.[4] This includes the company Gild, which uses analytics to predict who will be the best computer programmer, and the company Evolv, which focuses on hourly employees.[5] Gild has developed an algorithm that trolls through various data points to determine which of these items are associated with being a great programmer. Evolv evaluates personal characteristics to predict how well someone is likely to perform a job and also how long he or she is likely to hold that job.[6]

According to an article in *Fox Business,* the CEO of Yahoo!, Marissa Mayer, insists on approving every hire.[7] In this case, tools from human science could help Mayer substantially with her decision-making process. Absent the use of sophisticated analytics, there are potential downsides to Ms. Mayer's approach. The obvious is the potential for slowing the hiring process down to a crawl. In addition, there is considerable potential for biases to be present in her selection decisions. The potential for bias is actually exasperated because she tends to prefer to hire those who went to top-tier schools and prefers computer science majors over electrical engineers.[8] Tools such as those being developed by Gild and Evolv could assist Yahoo's CEO (along with virtually everyone else making section decisions) to make accurate, unbiased, and timely decisions.

4.1.5 Skills Shortages

Even during the depths of the recession, substantial skills gaps and vacancies existed throughout the United States and other developed economies. The shortage of technical talent was particularly acute. This may mean that more students should be pursuing technical degrees, or it may mean that that the technical degrees do not provide the skills needed by organizations. Everyone is better off if the matching of job requirements with specific knowledge and skills is clearly identified.

A multitude of online courses are available to anyone anywhere. It would not be difficult to develop a curriculum using free online course from places like MIT and Stanford for one of the hottest emerging jobs: Data Scientist. If you are sufficiently motivated you can become proficient in one of the most marketable jobs today. However, this is only part of the equation, the supply side. The other side, of course, is the demand side: organizations making it clear what specific skill set they are looking for. This is the role of workforce planning.

Workforce planning is a critical function for the success of the organization, but it is too often not done as well as it could be. Organizations may be too quick (or slow) to hire during an upturn and too quick to lay off upon a downturn. One of the biggest challenges I have run into time and again in my own professional life is having all the other resources readily available (such as financial and technical) but lacking the human capital that is ready and able to execute the plan. At this point in our very slow recovery, many organizations are seriously pondering the decision to hire or not to hire. They are loath to miss opportunities, but overstaffing is in no one's interest. Advanced analytics can assist with making a more accurate workforce headcount projection.

4.2 Workforce Planning, Talent Acquisition, and Decision Analytics

Workforce planning and talent acquisition are well suited for advanced analytics. Workforce planning consists of determining the current workforce situation, evaluating that against what is going on in the macro-environment, and making workforce adjustments (either reduce or increase head count). Advanced analytics can assist with making much more accurate planning projections.

It is possible to get an accurate read on the current situation of the firm and to determine the future needs of the organization. This requires a mechanism for effectively scanning the environment, in order to get an idea on the state of the economy, the workforce, and your organization's challenges and opportunities.

Substantial research provides evidence that getting the right employee is associated with higher productivity, greater profitability, lower employee turnover, and generally much better organizational outcomes. Arguably, who you decide to bring in to your company is an important decision (perhaps the most important). If you bring in the wrong people, not much else of what you do matters. Granted, depending on the country in which you reside, you may have a fair degree of flexibility to sever the employment relationship. Wherever you are, though, hiring and training employees takes much time and energy. So, the better your recruitment and selection decisions, the better performance outcomes and cost savings.

Traditionally, the selection decision has been heavily weighted toward the interview. However, this has been shown to be a poor predictor of future job performance. A number of other instruments are considerably more useful when making selection decisions, and this section focuses on where these instruments and current and emerging analytical tools complement one another. For instance, one tool increasingly used today and a good fit for developing and emerging technologies is the use of biographical data (or Bio data) for selection decisions.

The recruitment and selection process is one rife with potential biased decisions making. Two researchers recently found that when pictures are included with a curriculum vitae, as they are often in Europe and Asia, they found that attractive men were more likely to be invited in for an interview. The inverse applied for attractive women. The less attractive, the more likely you are to be invited. Bradley Ruffle and Ze'ev Shtudiner determined that this was not because attractive women were considered less intelligent, but rather because recruiters (who are generally female) are attempting to limit the competition.[9]

4.2.1 Workforce Planning and Predictive Analytics

The topic of workforce planning is one that brought me to the use of analytics to make better decisions. I became interested in the topic back in the late 1980s, when it was referred to as human resource planning. The person I worked with while interning at Honeywell had done influential work on the topic. For me, the topic pulled together a number of interesting subjects, including environmental scanning, a vision for the direction of the organization, and the utilization of tools and techniques to predict what skills, abilities, experiences, personal qualities, and knowledge would enable people to achieve organizational success.

Workforce planning, in particular, has a big impact on whether an organization has the bandwidth to respond to ever-changing business challenges and opportunities. Workforce planning, like all human capital management (HCM) decisions, has been viewed as part art and part science. I am clearly attempting to put as much science as possible into the decision-making process.

One of the more important and upfront decisions that has to be taken is how many employees do we need? Generally, organizations are notoriously bad at getting this number right; and it matters a lot. Having the right talent in the right place at the right time makes all the difference. Firms miss significant opportunities when they do not have the right employee in the right place at the right time.

Workforce planning consists of the following steps:

- Scanning the macro-environment
- Organizational strategic objectives
- Current workforce situation
- Projected workforce needs
- Analysis
- Action plan to fill gaps

4.2.2 When Is Workforce Planning Necessary?

This is a topic in where organizations can utilize organizational data to evaluate the impact of past recessions, downturns, or periods of fast economic growth on employee headcount. Looking back over the headcount trends during the economic cycle to evaluate appropriate headcount (in busy or not-so-busy times) will provide data to help in future headcount determination.

Workforce planning may be much more helpful and necessary (and difficult) in substantially dynamic environments. If the organization is experiencing predictable growth, and business as usual is expected to continue with fairly static employee turnover, a fairly uncomplicated workforce planning system is needed.[10] If the situation is a dynamic work environment in which there is uncertainty in the environment, there is a need for more sophisticated workforce planning methods.

4.2.3 Challenges with Forecasting

Daniel Kahneman recounts a story about his experiences with a curriculum planning group in Israel.[11] He provides a detailed story about how upon serving on this committee, he and the other committee members were confident that they were making good progress. Kahneman decided to check the assumptions that both he and the other members of the group maintained. Everyone in the group wrote down how long they thought it would take to write a book and develop a new curriculum. The estimate given by those present was somewhere between 1.5 years and 2.5 years, with the average being 2. It occurred to Daniel to ask one of the fellow group members, the dean of the School of Education and someone who had considerable experience with curriculum development, how long on average it took the other groups in which they had experience to complete the same tasks. According to Kahneman, the dean looked somewhat dismayed and said on average 7 years and that 40% did not complete the task at all. He then asked the dean to compare the skills of the current group with the skills of the other group. Apparently, the dean worked with some pretty high-skilled curriculum planners, because even with the future Nobel Prize winner in the group, he ranked the group as below average. In the end, it took 8 years to complete the book, and the curriculum was never used.

Kahneman saw this as one of the more formative events in his professional life. It had a substantial impact on his view of forecasting, which he and Amos Tversky labeled the *inside view* and the *outside view*.[12] The inside view is the one we initially assume when evaluating a potential outcome. For instance, until he took the time to reflect, the dean thought it would take only up to 2.5 years to complete the book. It was not until after reflecting on the other curriculum planning groups that a more realistic view emerged. Forecasting based on previous data or information from similar tasks and related outcomes can be considered the outside view.

The COWI consulting group and the academic Bent Flyvbjerg have taken this process and applied it to a variety of processes that involve forecasting (mostly estimates associated with costing projects). The process is called *reference class forecasting*, and it applies mostly to transportation policy and planning.[13] The process consists of the following steps:

(1) Identification of a relevant reference class of past, similar projects. The class must be broad enough to be statistically meaningful but narrow enough to be truly comparable with the specific project.

(2) Establishing a probability distribution for the selected reference class. This requires access to credible, empirical data for a sufficient number of projects within the reference class to make statistically meaningful conclusions.

(3) Comparing the specific project with the reference class distribution, to establish the most likely outcome for the specific project.[14] This might sound complicated, but it can be applied to a number of different forecasting issues that arise within HCM. In essence, this entails looking back at previous workforce planning numbers and evaluating to determine how close they are to actual.

What's more, experimentation can be undertaken. Seeing what happened during the last recession allows an organization to do a much better job of predicting the likely outcome associated with the next downturn, and how and when to start getting back in the game again. The same applies when things are going along well; this will provide you the information necessary so that you can know best when to start throttling back on hires.

It is true that when it comes to headcount and labor costs, the emphasis is on maximum flexibility. Two problems generally emerge when attempting to forecast future outcomes. One is *optimism bias*, and the second *strategic misrepresentation*. This means that the starting point for this question (optimal workforce planning) is getting the model right. What factors go in to predicting the kind of knowledge skills and abilities we will need to carry out the strategic objectives of the organization?

For examples of these and other tools, please go to: Decision AnalyticsInc.com.

4.2.4 External Big Data and Employee Recruitment and Selection

One of the primary new sources of data for selection and recruitment is social media. There is an explosive interest in the potential predictive power of social analytics. This data is being used to predict social uprisings and to target consumer preferences. IARPA, the Informatics branch of DARPA, recently held a competition of fund research associated with determining the optimal utilization of social media.

Social analytics are already being used extensively within the marketing function, with much of this evolving around the use of sentiment analysis to examine and determine how consumers or potential consumers feel about a specific service or product. Organizations are also increasingly using social media to assist in recruitment efforts and to gauge the morale of the organization.

Other organizations are also providing very valuable data that can be utilized to make more accurate headcount and selection decisions. For instance, Glassdoor is a company that provides good background information into what is being said about other companies.[15] Founded in 2007 by Richard Barton, Robert Hohman, and Tim Besse, Glassdoor provides information on job postings for more than 150,000 companies across 100 countries. They provide salary information, CEO ratings, and impressions of the work environment from current and former employees.

There are challenges associated with the use of social analytics. The issue of privacy is a serious issue. Data privacy laws are in place in Europe, and the issue can be contentious in the United States. It is becoming increasingly common for interviewers to ask for passwords to gain access to social media content.[16] This has become pervasive enough that state legislatures are proposing bills to prevent employers from discriminating against employees who refuse to give access to their social media information.[17]

4.3 Human Science and Selection and Promotions Decisions

The overriding question here is: What process allows us to predict the ideal employee. Clearly, this largely depends on the type of employee you are looking for.

One of the more promising tools to assist with selection and promotions decisions is the use of biographical data (Bio data). This information is based largely on identifying specific characteristics that ultimately predict job success. Google has been using this technique to assist with hiring decisions for some years.[18] There is evidence that Bio data surveys are better predictor of future performance than, say, the job interview.

You'll recall my earlier example of the excellent check-out person I encountered. In the case of that grocery store chain, they would administer a survey to him that would identify characteristics and attributes, then administer a survey to prospective candidates evaluating for the same qualities. This can all be done online and very cost effectively.

4.3.1 *What We Have to Learn from the Use of Advanced Analytics for Player Selection in Professional Sports*

Some of you may have seen the movie *Moneyball* starring Brad Pitt, Jonah Hill, and Philip Seymour Hoffman. The book the movie is based on, *Moneyball: The Art of Winning an Unfair Game,* was written by Michael Lewis. It is the story of Billy Beane, the then general manager of Major League Baseball's Oakland A's. Beane's team had the third smallest payroll in the MBL, so he used analytics to provide his team with a winning advantage. At the time, in 2002, the use of analytics in sports was considered radical, even foolish. Now, the use of analytics to make decisions within sports is widespread. Since 2005, MIT has held a Sports Analytics Conference, and it has grown in size and influence.[19] The conference in 2012 had representatives from 73 professional teams from 6 sports.[20] Professional sports, with the tradition of keeping player statistics, make an ideal candidate for the use of analytics in decision making. Baseball, in particular, with its 162 regular season games, provides an ample sample size for rigorous analysis (more so than the data provided by the 82 games in basketball or the 16 in football).

The movie *Moneyball* has done much to bring analytics into popular consciousness. While there is no question that the use of analytics has helped to put predictive analytics on the radar for many, much of what is being accomplished in the professional sports arena is an attempt to do exactly what firms are spending a tremendous amount of time doing. They are attempting to predict who will be first-rate employees. The crux of the matter is determining which characteristics are actually associated with superior performance.

As those who saw *Moneyball* may remember, traditional analytics did not predict success. (In the case of the Oakland A's, that would be winning games.) This is an important lesson that can be learned from the use of analytics: The factors that are actually associated with predicting success are usually much broader than traditionally thought.

The same hard work to establish what is actually associated with success in your particular organization is just as critical. For example, you often hear the phrase "we only hire the best people." It should read like this instead: We only hire the best person for our specific organization and situation. An example is that many organizations now recognize the value of hiring people who are also willing and able to work collaboratively.

Many of the advances associated with increased accuracy of recruitment and selection are due to more accurate models of what ultimately impacts enterprise success. Therefore, it is critical that firms are clear on what is associated with success in their specific organization and follow this up with an appropriate recruitment, selection, incentive, and performance and talent management programs.

We have a lot to learn from professional sports teams. Keep in mind a couple of critical factors here. Most sports, except golf and singles tennis, epitomize a team production function. Of course, there can be a star center or a great shortstop or quarterback who makes a big difference; however, it is impossible to win alone. The same obviously applies when attempting to achieve organizational goals.

4.3.2 Biases and the Selection Decision

Few decisions in organizations are more susceptible to bias than the selection decision. In March 2013, the magazine *Nature* ran a special issue on the inequity female scientists face. The results are quite startling. Women are much less likely to get hired, promoted, receive grants, or get tenure, even after controlling for all other factors such as labor market participation (for instance, taking time off), experience, and education.

The selection decision is one of the most critical aspects of the employment decision and also is subject to considerable downside risk. Traditional hiring practices come with a number of potential downsides. There is the *halo effect* and the *similar-to-me* bias, neither of which can influence an algorithm. To see the impact of technological advances in HCM decision making, you just have a look at Google patents.[21] Doing an open search on "employee selection" returns 17,300 sites. The use of technology to assist with many of these appears to be focused on the use of technology to enhance selection decisions. Many companies are starting to use advanced analytics for the selection and recruitment decisions. This is one function where there is quite a lot of scope for the utilization of these technologies to make better decisions.

4.3.3 Selection Tools: Augmented Biographical Survey

Using bio data as a selection instrument consists of using personal history as a predictor of future job performance.[22] Making selection decisions based on bio data has a long history.[23] In a journal article published in 1922, Dorothy Goldsmith finds the approach to be useful when attempting to predict the success of salesmen.[24] This technique has been shown to be effective and is viewed by researchers as one of the most effective tools for predicting successful future job performance.[25] However, it is not being used extensively. In a survey of HR professionals, comparing 11 different selection devices (including personal hunches), bio data ranked tenth in terms of perceived validity, ninth for practicality, and tenth for legality.[26] James Breaugh challenges these perceptions and states that the use of bio data for selection decision should be more widely used.

One of the worst predictors of employment success is the job interview, and job testing is not much better. You might be able to nail the GRE, but you might lack the proverbial "fire in the belly." Aaron Rogers, the quarterback of the Green Bay Packers (Super Bowl winners in 2010), started off in a community college, and he could not get a scholarship. He played and he played well; he had something to prove, and he constantly reminds himself of those days.

The use of bio data is a straightforward: Determine successful characteristics of current job holders and determine the relationship of these characteristics to job performance. Prospective job candidates are then screened for these characteristics.

The use of the bio data it allows for the inclusion of candidates who may have been screened out using traditional measures.[27] An algorithm allows for an evaluation of a much broader set of characteristics, and they also avoid the potential downsides human decision makers often exhibit.

In the first instance, start by identifying those behaviors, characteristics, and activities that lead to success on the job. Ultimately, this also needs to be mapped to how job success leads to organizational success. At this point, there is also a role for Kahnman's "thinking fast." Of course, I say this with my standard warning against all the biases associated with a decision like this. However, a manager or executive with long experience and expertise may well have a good intuition about someone.

Advanced analytics in the form of predictive modeling is ideally suited for the use of bio data. Analytics can go considerably beyond the straightforward who-to-hire question. We can use these techniques to help reduce or eliminate discrimination and even wage inequality.

4.3.4 Challenges with the Use of Bio Data

There is, however, scope for problems associated with the use of bio data instruments. For instance, there is concern that the use of bio data tools may identify negative characteristics associated with performance (such as addictive tendencies) or result in less diversity by perpetuating a *similar-to-me* bias.

These are risks with these two issues and another example of where seasoned human expertise plays a critical role. If the recommended candidates are trending toward too little diversity, adjustments can be made. In addition, the tool should be carefully validated so that it accurately reflects *actual* job tasks and also attributes that accurately predict success at those tasks.

As discussed, any kind of bias is suboptimal when making selection decisions, and the stronger the connection between attributes or characteristics and performance outcomes, the greater the validity of the selection instrument. A well designed bio data instrument should provide a strong connection between attributes and performance, eliminating all other factors from consideration. Effort should go into verifying the measures of these characteristics and attributes and their relationship to performance. Purely technically, bio data should provide a direct data-based connection. However, selection decisions will ultimately be made by someone or ones. Those ultimate decision makers need to be aware of their potential for bias and guard against it. If in doubt, like flight instructors tell pilots working toward obtaining an Instrument Rating (flying by instruments alone), trust what the instruments are telling you. If you have put the time in to make a robust validated instrument, the same applies here.

4.4   Applications of Human Science to Selection Decisions

4.4.1 *The Application of Expert Intuition to Selection and Promotion Decisions*

There is room for well-seasoned professional intuition when it comes to selection and promotions decisions; however, there is also substantial room for biased judgments. Making judgments about whether someone is a good fit with the organization and the team often requires expert intuition; however, tools from advanced analytics can help eliminate other extraneous factors.

4.4.2 Applied Game Theory and Selection Decisions

In order for cooperation to emerge it requires the same employees. Hiring and promotion decisions should include predictive analytics on the likelihood of the employee staying with the organization.

4.4.3 Deep Q&A Expert Systems and Selection Decisions

Certainly, a Watson-like expert system can assist with selection decisions. A database can be built containing Bio data and the track record of the performance of hires and promotions. This data can be used to predict the likely success of new hires and promotions. In addition, these systems can be used to make recommendations regarding what developmental experiences are needed by employees.

4.4.4 Predictive Modeling and Selections Decisions

Characteristics and attributes predicting the ideal employee for your organization can be built using a combination of Bio data and performance data. These techniques can also be used to predict future number of employees needed, what attributes and characteristics make for a great executive, actuary, sales clerk, teacher, etc. Information from these models can be used to identify developmental needs.

4.4.5 Applied Econometric and Machine Learning Techniques

There are a number of tools and techniques from econometrics and A.I./Machine Learning that can be used to make better selection decisions.

- **Multiple Regression Techniques:** Multiple regression techniques can be used to assess impact. It can be used to determine the impact on performance associated with the introduction of a new policy or program.

- **Decision Trees:** Essentially a graph or model depicting steps to a decision. This can be used to provide evidence-based recommendations on the type of developmental experience an potential executive should obtain prior to promotion.

- **Monte Carlo Simulation:** This consists of using computation algorithms to arrive at probability distributions, allowing determination of the likelihood that a particular intervention (such as putting in a child care facility) will have on employee turnover.

5

Human Science and Incentives

5.1 Human Science and Incentives

Daniel Ariely, the author of *Predictably Irrational*, is one of the top behavioral economists working today. In a TED talk in 2012, he discussed some of his research associated with motivation and work.[1] In this talk, he recounts a presentation he gave at a major software company in Seattle. His presentation was to 200 software engineers who had over the previous two years been charged with coming up with the "next big thing." The week before Ariely's talk, the COO had met with the engineers and told them to stop working on the project. According to Ariely, the group of engineers he spoke to that day were some of the most depressed people he had ever encountered. The research he discussed was on work, meaning, and motivation and spoke directly to why these engineers were so disheartened. Ariely's research found that a focus on pecuniary (financial) rewards is misdirected; the focus should be on making work rewarding by making it meaningful and challenging—and when done well, acknowledged and recognized.

The topic of incentives and motivation is one in which the new understanding of human science has substantial significance. If we are not just profit-maximizing cyborgs, how exactly are we to be motivated? Evidence indicates that the way we have been compensating people can do more harm than good. Consider, for example, the financial crisis. All one had to do was look at the way in which compensation was structured at financial institutions to see that a financial crisis was eminent.[2] Incentive contracts for investment bankers provided an incentive to take extreme risks.[3]

I do not think it is an overstatement to say that one of the most critical issues facing organizations today (and many economies) is the establishment of a robust connection between rewards and performance. Take, for example, the issue of executive compensation. Much evidence supports a disconnection between executive rewards and performance.[4] Executive compensation is often set as a function of the power of the executive rather than performance of the firm.[5] The disconnection between rewards and performance extends well beyond those who occupy the executive suite. Research has shown substantial pay differences based on gender alone.[6] And gender pay bias is only one form of wage discrimination; age and race are associated with biased decision practices, but *not* with job performance. Again, if we need to be reminded why this matters, it matters because it matters to human capital. Treating people with bias will *cause* disengagement (lower morale, lower productivity, higher turnover), ultimately resulting in suboptimal organizational performance.

In addition, the wages of those in the middle class have been mostly flat or declining over the past 30 years.[7] This occurred during the same period that company profits were soaring. The flat real income growth applies to not only manufacturing and service workers, but also in varying degrees to professionals including teachers, airline pilots, nurses, and so on. Wage inequality undermines organizational effectiveness, and, more broadly, economic prosperity. This is no small thing. In the United States, consumer spending drives 70% of the economic activity. If we want growth, we need to more accurately allocate profits to those responsible for making them. This includes making a strong line-of-sight connection between rewards and performance, but it also means making informed decision about what incentive practice to use. For instance, it may mean that high-performing individuals and teams of store check-out clerks and hotel room cleaners should be getting stock options, but top executives should not.

There are a number of roles here for human science. The use of analytics can result in the establishment of a more robust connection between performance and rewards, not only for executives but for everyone in the organization. There is also the opportunity to include more pertinent information when developing incentive schemes. No two people's situation or preferences are identical, and yet organizations reward entire job families in exactly the same manner. Organizations have relied too heavily on benchmarking data (and inaccurate assumptions about what motivates people), virtually ignoring individual motivational profiles. Treating everyone in precisely the same manner has almost certainly led to suboptimal performance outcomes. As detailed in Chapter 4, "Human Science and Selection Decisions," a number of companies are applying human science to questions related to employee selection. However, applying these new developments to incentive contracts and performance management decisions is much less well developed.

I believe any discussion about selection decisions has to also include incentives, and vice versa. If you are attempting to choose people who will help make your organization thrive, that means you want someone who is motivated and engaged. You will want to keep them engaged, and the only way that will be accomplished is if you determine what motivates them and their team.

When I use the term "incentives," I use it broadly, using a total compensation approach that includes both pecuniary (that is, base salary, bonus, and so on) and non-pecuniary (that is, organizational culture and brand) incentives. Earlier I discussed the privately held analytic software company SAS. Their pecuniary components of their incentives are a small part of a much larger "total compensation" approach. In many ways, this is a much more optimal way in which to structure incentives. SAS provides day care, in-house social workers, and a health club. These components of total compensation are more in-line with how humans, as opposed to econs, are motivated.

To access tools associated with this book, visit my site at Decision AnalyticsInc.com.

5.1.1 *Incentives, Motivation, and Human Science*

The standard underlying motivational assumption associated with incentives is that of rationality and profit maximization—that people evaluate incentives typically based on a short-term, self-centered, income-maximizing framework. This is not the entire picture, and with the help of advanced analytics, we can develop incentive contracts that focus on what really motivates people.

As with selection decisions, compensation decisions are prone to biased decision making. Getting the incentives wrong can lead to human capital focusing on the wrong things and to employee morale and engagement problems, employee turnover, or, as some would argue, to the collapse of an organization or an entire economy.[8]

Compensation is clearly a key business decision and impacts the success of the organization. Executive compensation is a divisive topic, and getting incentive contracts right for executives (closely aligning pay and organizational performance) is critical for the well-being of the organization. However, establishing a pay-for-performance connection is important at all levels in the organization, not only the executive level.

A challenge in compensation that advanced analytics can address is overdependence on benchmarking to establish total compensation packages. One of the more beneficial aspects of advanced analytics is that it allows for the inclusion of a broader amount of information when designing incentive contracts. Not only can market data be included, but also information about what actually motivates the specific individual and team.

Representatives from one well-known organization sit down with employees when they are hired and ask them how they would like to be paid. Of course, at that point, discussions associated with base salary and any variable pay and benefits have already been discussed, but employees have room to "tailor" their compensation to their own preferences. This sort of individual tailoring of compensation may strike you as odd; it seemed strange to me when I first heard about it. After all, organizations usually dictate the various components of compensation. The *individualization* of incentives is exactly what advanced analytics is well suited for. One size does not fit all; what motivates me might not motive you, and our situations certainly differ. This again goes back to the issue of asymmetric or private information. The individual has information about preferences, but the organization also has asymmetric information about what they would like to see accomplished. Combining the two in a manner that maximizes both parties' utility is the ideal.

5.1.2 Incentive Contracts

In the standard economic approach, firms develop incentive contracts for employees because organizations do not know how hard employees can work, so they need to incur costs in the form of incentive contracts in order to keep employees in line. Otherwise employees might shirk duties or engage in *moral hazard*, self-interested misbehavior.

One approach to compensation is to compensate people based on their marginal revenue product or their bottom-line impact on organizational performance.[9] The problem with this is that it is difficult to determine individual (team or group) contribution to organizational performance.

Piece rates are viewed as one of the more efficient forms of incentives, and they do have a strong incentive effect. Piece rates compensate based on the quantity of goods produced. The challenge with this form of incentive is when you reward based on quantity, you often see a sacrifice in quality.

Generally, incentive schemes in organizations are based on a tournament model and focus on individual contribution. We come by the tournament model honestly because most organizations are hierarchical, with much of the decision-making authority residing with those at the top. Hierarchies with consolidated decision-making authority at the top of the organization are an efficient organizational design if those in the executive suite have perfect information and perform all the tasks of the organization.

Tournament-structured compensation can produce inefficient behaviors. This incentive contract structure can promote mistrust and animosity between employees. Tournament incentive structures may provide an incentive for employees of one department to withhold information that would have been helpful to those in another. The entire organization loses out when individuals and teams are rewarded for not sharing potentially value creating information.

Much of the research associated with incentive compensation has been has been done using research from sports. As a long-time fan of the Green Bay Packers (and being one of 363,948 "owners"),[10] I am certainly interested in getting the incentives right in our sports teams. However, the problem has been that the findings for sports (specifically tournament compensation) have been extrapolated to compensation in organizations, and this can be problematic. As covered in Chapter 4, advanced analytics has been applied to selection decisions in sports, but has not yet been applied in the same way to incentives for athletes and team success. Research has found benefits associated with tournament pay (the winner-takes-all philosophy) for individual athletic performance; however, there is not much research evaluating incentives and the success of the team as a whole. Yes, a Michael Jordan can make or break a team (the typical NBA team has a roster of 15 players, not the 500, 5,000, or 50,000 found in organizations), but not even Jordan was an island. Without Dennis Rodman pulling down all those rebounds, Jordan does not get the ball and the shot. As in organizations, sporting teams may benefit substantially from spending more time getting not only individual, but also group and team incentive compensation, right.

5.1.3 Collaboration and Tournament Compensation Do Not Go Together

We do not have to look any further than the Tour de France to find a problem with tournament compensation. This is an example of how the power of tournament-based incentives can promote suboptimal non-value maximizing behaviors. Lance Armstrong embodies the problem with tournaments perfectly. By his own admission, he cheated and lied. We do not like folks who cheat; however, tournament-based incentives can provide an incentive to do just that.

Contrast Armstrong's behavior's with the behaviors of one of the most decorated soldiers in World War II: Audie Murphy. He was awarded the Medal of Honor at age 19 and was also awarded military honors in both France and Belgium. His entire life, Murphy insisted that the awards should have been given not to him individually, but rather to his entire military unit.[11]

If tournament compensation does not work, or has too many potential downsides, what kind of incentive schemes do work and when? If you see the value in collaboration and cooperation within your organization, including team and group incentives are necessary.

5.1.4 We Get What We Pay For

We should not underestimate the importance of establishing and maintaining a strong and credible connection between compensation and performance. Many serious organizational and social problems result directly from poorly designed incentive schemes. The near collapse of the financial system is an example; we got exactly what we paid for. Bankers across the globe were rewarded for swinging for the fences, the rating agencies were compensated by those who they were meant to regulate, and banks were aware that any gains were theirs to keep, but excessive losses would be borne by others.

Back when I was graduating from college, there were those who thought IBM was the top place to go work. One of the reasons everyone wanted to work for IBM was because the pay was higher there than pretty much anyone else. It was thought this attracted the top people. This pay practice is referred to as efficiency wage.

The notion of efficiency wage states that if you pay above market rate, you attract the best talent. You will work extra hard if you have been "gifted" a higher salary.[12] Of course, all the gifting was almost not enough to save Big Blue, which nearly crashed and burned. Yes, they hired from the top schools those with the highest GPAs, but it might not have been the most optimal way in which to attract and incent people. The notion of efficiency wages, with its focus on financial rewards alone, may not motivate maximum value creation from human capital.

In addition to the larger macro-level issues, a number of significant micro-influences are equally problematic. One of the biggest challenges with compensation is the problem of internal and external equity. For example, merit pay has long had a credibility problem because of the perceived, and frequently real, subjectivity that is often a part of the review process. Done correctly, the use of advanced analytics can substantially reduce subjectivity associated with merit-based compensation decisions.

Clearly, from an organizational performance perspective, rewards make a significant impact on the success of an organization—starting at the executive level and moving through the ranks of the organization. Generally, the closer one can get to making a strong connection between pay and performance, the more likely he or she is to see the compensation approach as being equitable and reasonable.

5.2 Human Science and Motivation

When I first started writing this book, my focus was squarely on the use of advanced analytics because organizations will be more successful and make more money if they start making better and less biased hiring and compensation decisions, and this remains accurate. However, as the process went on, it also became apparent that by making more accurate selection and pay decisions on the micro-level, we are chipping away at what many believe to be the two largest macro-level social issues of our time; inequality of opportunity and inequality of wages. This book, and the related software we are developing, became even more interesting and engaging. It is starting to be better understood that meaningful work is as important if not more important than financial rewards.

In the introduction to this section, I mentioned a talk that Daniel Ariely gave to a group of software engineers in Seattle. In the research he presented to the software engineers that day, Ariely was interested in the relationship between financial rewards, meaning and effort. In order to test these notions, he and his collaborators developed a test in which participants would, for a financial reward, assemble LEGO Bionicles (I didn't know what those were either; sort of like miniature robots). They received $3.00 for the first Bionicle, decreasing by 30 cents each time they built one—for example, $2.70 for the second one, $2.40 for the third, and so on. In the first round of this experiment (referred to as the "meaningful condition"), Ariely and his colleagues would watch the participant make the Bionicle, place it under the table, give them the materials to make another, and so on. The average participant constructed 11. In the second experiment (they referred to it as the "Sisyphus condition," referring to the king who was punished by God to roll a rock up a hill for eternity only to watch it roll back down right before it got to the top), they took the Bionicle that the participant had just assembled and disassembled it right in front of them. In the Sisyphus condition, they only built 7 on average.

They then described the experiment to a new group of participants, without actually having them build Bionicles, and asked them to speculate on what they thought would be the outcome. The average participant speculated that 8 would be built in the meaningful condition and 7 during the Sisyphus condition. They got the direction correct, but not the magnitude.

They also factored in a participant's love for LEGOs; that is, some people just love building things with LEGOs, so presumably the greater the love for LEGOs, the more they would build. This is exactly what they found in the meaningful condition: a very strong relationship between intrinsic satisfaction and the number of Bionicles built. In the Sisyphus condition, there was no correlation between the number of Bionicles built and intrinsic satisfaction. Apparently, Ariely concludes, any joy or satisfaction associated with building LEGOs was crushed when the Bionicles were taken apart right in front of them.

What this is telling us is that when we are designing incentive contracts, the financial element is only part of the story and may well not even be the most interesting part. This will of course vary by person and by industry and job and location; however, contributing to something meaningful and being recognized are powerful motivators.

When it comes to designing incentive contracts that include these motivational components, expert intuition can play a very important role. It is hard to imagine that the executive at the large software company in Seattle that delivered the bad news to the software engineers about their project would leave everyone hanging. Here you have 200 software engineers demotivated and underutilized. As Ariely points out, this had an impact on productivity and could have easily led to employee turnover. Their financial compensation was probably not impacted, but the significance of their work was completely undermined.

What does this aspect of human science have to do with advanced analytics? If you are attempting to accurately *predict* how people are going to respond to a new policy, practice, or some other action, it is important to understand an impacting effort and engagement is about more than just money.

5.3 Performance Management

The objective of performance management systems is to align the individual (and the team) activities with organizational goals. Often, however, a long list of secondary factors influences performance management decisions. Performance management decisions are subject to a wide range of biases and information asymmetries. Advanced analytics can provide a mechanism to eliminate many of the factors influencing evaluator bias. Performance management is defined as follows:

> The means through which managers ensure that employee's activities and outputs are congruent with the organization's goals.[13]

The focus of much of strategic HCM is the alignment of HCM practices and policies with business objectives. For policies and practices to have an impact on performance, they need to ultimately influence value-creating employee behaviors and activities.

First, you want to determine the right set of policies and practices in your specific situation. Unfortunately, performance management practices are often handed down because this is what was always done, or it is what the firm next door is doing. Keep in mind that the overall objective is employee engagement—getting everyone on the same page, excited, and motivated to carry out the objectives of the organization.

Performance management provides the following functions:

- Help determine which performance management and incentive system to put into place

- Develop a line-of-sight connection between individual and team performance and organizational objectives
- Evaluate the effectiveness of the policies and practices

5.3.1 Biases Impacting Performance Management and Compensation Decisions

A challenge that organizations encounter is one of managing performance well. Part of the issue is also a problem with the *model* (that is, determining which factors are associated with superior performance). There are a broad range of factors, including the following:

- Skills, abilities, knowledge, and individual characteristics
- Organizational characteristics and business objectives
- External and internal conditions and constraints[14]

Getting performance management right matters; employee engagement and satisfaction is associated with superior business outcomes.[15] However, numerous factors conspire against the accurate evaluation of performance. Of all the HCM-related activities, one that certainly has much downside potential for biased decisions is performance management. Some argue that evaluators are inconsistent and that there is a high degree of subjectivity in such evaluation.[16]

- **Appraisal politics:** This is more common and more problematic than most other forms of biases. In the case of appraisal politics, evaluators consciously distort ratings to achieve individual or other division or company goals.
- **Similar to me bias:** We generally view ourselves as being competent and effective; so if we find someone who is very much like us, we are more prone to positively evaluate and reward that person.

- **Halo and horn effect:** This bias occurs when a rater ascribes one positive quality to all qualities. The inverse is the horn effect, when a negative quality is ascribed across all other characteristics.

Few topics have the potential to be more contentious within an organization than decisions related to compensation rewards. It can be a process that is rife with many of the biases outlined in Chapter 1, "Challenges and Opportunities with Optimal Decision Making and How Advanced Analytics Can Help." For instance, merit pay has long been considered problematic because it was thought to be prone to subjectivity bias. (That is, those who were liked by the boss were given higher bonuses than those who were not.) It is safe to say that there are many, many ways to get compensation wrong, and numerous factors often go into the compensation decision.

Both Gartner and Forrester Research[17] evaluate a variety of different tools to assist with total compensation decisions. There are tools that can assist with the administration of compensation; however, the application of more advanced tools to these problems is less well developed.

5.3.2 Strategy Maps and Performance Management

In the previous section, "5.2 Human Science and Motivation," I discussed how the new human science recognizes that we are not only about income or profit maximization, but we also are looking for our work to have significance and meaning. In this section, I will be discussing how some tools can assist us with developing better connections between our decisions and effort and between organizational performance and outcomes. This will ultimately result in a more equitable dispersion of rewards.

I have already spent some time discussing the Balance Scorecard, and this is certainly a tool that can be used to better reward executives. There are a number of different automated scorecards available that go a long way toward establishing a line sight connection between performance and individual and team behaviors and activities.

Certainly in the case of executives, all of the data is readily available to link their decisions on capital expenditures, strategic initiatives, and execution to operational and financial outcomes. Furthermore, there are excellent performance management tools such as IBM CFO Performance Dashboard or SAS Strategy Management that can provide all the necessary data.

Strategy maps can provide a variety of metrics that represent operational outcomes. It is possible to see how these metrics co-vary relative to one another, and assuming the system maintains historical metrics, it is possible to do what we discussed in Chapter 3; we are able to establish cause and effect through the use of panel data.

In addition, dashboards and scorecards can provide tools to help identify relationships between metrics and performance, including human capital metrics such as labor costs, employee turnover, and employee morale. As I mentioned earlier, Forrester Research and Gartner Inc. provide an excellent review of all these and other products.

5.4 Applying Human Science to Incentive Contracts

5.4.1 Irrational, Cooperative, and Looking for Meaning

By focusing primarily on financial rewards, incentive contracts mostly miss the mark. Most of us like working together, doing challenging but meaningful work, and being recognized when we do well. The underlying assumption of rationality and profit-maximization in incentive contracts is incomplete. Tournament-based incentives force individualized, non-cooperative, winner-take-all behaviors that fail to maximize value creation in collaborative organizations. To maximize value, organizations need to develop incentive contracts that promote cooperation and collaboration and recognize both team and individual accomplishments.

5.4.2 *Complexity Theory and Incentive Contracts*

The Santa Fe Institute, founded in 1984 in (you can probably guess where) Santa Fe, New Mexico, is a very interesting research center.[18] The main focus of the Institute is complexity theory. Its researchers include physicists, economists, computer scientists, and fiction writers (the author Cormac McCarthy, author of *The Road* is based there). They were doing big data research way before it was cool. They attempt to model and predict the actions of individuals and groups, exactly what we are attempting to do. They have applied their work to such things as predicting movements of the financial markets and the likelihood of terrorist attacks. They have also done much work in "Agent-based Modeling," allowing for non-rational responses of individual agents. These very sophisticated models could be used to predict individual and group behaviors in organizations using various individual and group incentives.

5.4.3 *The Application of Expert Intuition to Incentive and Motivation Issues*

When it comes to merit pay or bonus payments, there is much room for biases to enter in the decision process, so "gut" decision should be used with caution. However, when it comes to determination of what will motivate or demotivate an individual or a team, there is much more room for intuition to play role. With stock options, for example, due to the vesting requirement, many of the positive effects on performance may be related to reduced turnover, but paying all employees in the same manner as executives with a company-wide incentive may well positively impact engagement and promote collaboration.

It is also possible to build mechanisms for factoring in expert judgment into the tools themselves, as in Dr. Virginia Apgar's test to evaluate the health of a newborn. She came up with the important variables, and it is an expert that is assessing the newborn. The same kind of "weighting" used in the Apgar test can be incorporated into data-driven decisions related to selection and incentive decisions.

5.4.4 Applied Game Theory and Incentive Contracts

I have explained the Prisoners Dilemma, which is an important element of game theory, in an earlier chapter. Another assumption is that in order to arrive at a cooperative solution, the "game" needs to be played over and over again. What this assumes is that the agents (employees) will be consistent (they will not quit) in order for this cooperative solution to eventually emerge. Practically speaking, if our organization would benefit substantially from cooperation and collaboration, then keeping the same employees is important. Having high employee turnover means that there is less likelihood that employees will ever establish a stable cooperative equilibrium. They need to establish the necessary history (bonds, trust) with each other in order to realize the full benefits of collaboration. This further implies that incentive contracts that have a strong employee retention effect (that is, a vesting requirement) are advisable where cooperation is beneficial.

5.4.5 Deep Q & A Expert Systems and Incentive Contract Decisions

Much like with selection decisions, the use of a "Watson-like" Expert System could provide very useful information and intelligence on what incentives to use when. It could provide evidence-based recommendations for both types and forms of specific incentives, drawing from a database containing research and data on a broad range of incentive contract options. Information on the organization, the individual, and the executive-level team could be included, providing recommendations based on the specific set of circumstances.

5.4.6 Predictive Modeling and Incentive Contracts

The same question asked in the last chapter (what predicts a great employee) is essentially the same one we are asking here. What predicts the optimal incentive contact for a cowboy, a physician, an executive? Complicating matters when it comes to determining optimal incentive contracts is that we are using a broad definition of incentives with an overall focus on what is it that motivates the individual, the team, and the organization as a whole to superior performance. In addition, we can also include both employer and employee preferences (or characteristics).

It is possible to obtain predictions on how teams, departments, and divisions will respond to prospective changes in incentives. Agent-based modeling provides an ideal mechanism for attributing for "non-rationale" responses by individual agents. Most models assume "rational" responses, which we know is not how humans actually act.

5.4.7 Applied Econometric and Machine Learning Techniques

There are a number of tools and techniques from econometrics and A.I./Machine Learning that have direct application to problems encountered in HCM. At least a partial list includes the following:

- **Multiple Regression Techniques:** Multiple regression techniques are the workhorse of much of analytics. They can be used to determine the impact on performance associated with the introduction of a new incentive scheme.

- **Decision Trees:** Essentially a graph or model depicting steps to a decision. This can be used to provide evidence-based recommendations on, for example, who should receive restricted stock and how much.

- **Monte Claro Simulation:** This consists of using computation algorithms to arrive at probability distributions or optimizations or calculate a solution to a differential equation. This technique could be used assess the probability of someone resigning.

- **Neural Nets:** Are used to model complex relationships between variables. Can be used to model probable outcomes in groups.

- **Linear and Non-Linear Programming:** Techniques using mathematical optimization to determine most efficient outcome. Used to determine most cost-effective payment package.

5.5 Application of Human Science to Specific Incentive Issues

5.5.1 Executive Compensation

As I discussed, one of the most highly charged organizational topics of the past 30 years has been the issue of executive compensation. For a time, it was thought that executives should hold a "meaningful" stake in the company, which led to the distribution of a substantial number of shares to executives. There has been substantial criticism that the stock gains had little to do with the actual performance of the executive. More recently, there is the back-dating scandal in which stock grant dates were "back dated" to when the stock value was at its lowest, ensuring the highest possible appreciation. Compensation consultants have also been criticized for adding to the problem by ratcheting up compensation for executives.

In the book *Pay Without Performance,* Lucian Bebchuk and Jesse Fried provide a convincing argument that the determination of executive compensation is largely a function of executive power.[19] Though the corporate board sets the compensation level, the CEO may still have considerable influence (depending on how much power he or she has) over the compensation package. This by definition means that these executives are receiving a disproportionate amount of the profits, which means, quite frankly, they are literally taking someone else's earnings. The closer we can link pay to actual performance, the more fair and accurate the dispersion of profits. The use of analytics in the decision-making process can assist in eliminating any of the influences not directly associated with actual performance.

By applying advanced analytics to executive compensation, we can accurately evaluate historical performance to determine the maximum effectiveness of the compensation package. One of the most promising techniques is the use of indexing compensation against peer companies to determine the level of impact associated with a particular payment package for executives.

A significant amount of research provides information on what works when. This research could be included in an expert system and provide evidence-based research on what incentive approach to use when and where. Having a "Watson-like" expert system would allow for making evidence-based recommendations on components of incentive and motivational components appropriate for the executive and the organization.

With the use of predictive modeling, based on insights from the new human science, we can go a long way toward predicting the desired outcomes. This would entail including organizational and individual characteristics, as well as organizational and individual objectives. There are numerous data sources available that would enable one to develop and experiment across a broad range of different incentive schemes at the executive level. The Edgar database is publically available data maintained by the Security and Exchange Commission that contains detailed compensation data on every publicly traded company in the United States. This free data source provides compensation data on the top five highest paid individuals in every publicly traded company. In addition to the data on executive compensation, there is also data associated with the financial performance of these firms. Here is all the data needed to conduct a very rigorous analysis of what works in executive compensation and what does not. The same data is commercially available through S&P Execucomp and through the executive compensation information provider Equilar.

One of the more informed means of compensating executives is through the use of indexation. This comprises evaluating the performance of the executives based on how well they do in comparison to an index comprised of peers or even the S&P 500. Though this is often considered relative to the top executives, this indexation should comprise not only the CEO compensation, but also the entire executive team.

In addition, most firms will also have detailed strategic and operational outcomes. All of these data sources can be organized in order to develop. The ERP systems will almost always include the data necessary in order to evaluate the performance of the top executives.

5.5.2 *Other Possible Human Science Incentive Applications*

5.5.2.1 *Low Wage Low Skill Workers*

Earlier, I discussed my experience with the checkout person where I do my grocery shopping. Check-out people, along with most service sector employees, fall into the category of "low wage low skill." They are often in direct contact with customers, which essentially makes them the "face" of the company. Also, by merit of their proximity to the products and consumer, they have access to information and intelligence that those many layers up do not. This information is valuable, and there should be an incentive to share and/or act on it.

The new human science would suggest that this group may be under-rewarded financially for their contribution, and would be excellent candidates for team or company-wide incentives in order to provide incentives to share information on customer preferences.

5.5.2.2 Merit Pay and Teachers

I believe most would agree that teachers play a crucial role in all societies. The impact they have on individual and cumulative human capital can be quantified, it adds-up to the aggregate output knowledge-based organizations. Motivating and retaining high-quality teachers is essential for the wellbeing of an economy.

Here too the focus on pecuniary rewards may be at least partially misdirected. Developing a motivation profile and a reward system that motivates continued superior performance is critical.

5.5.2.3 Incentives for Physicians

One place we should endeavor to get it right is with healthcare workers. The neoclassical view held that the highest ability would sort to jobs with the highest income. This is one of the reasons why physicians are paid so well in the United States; we want those with the highest ability to become doctors.

The World Health Organization ranked 191 countries on the quality of their healthcare, including costs. The United States spends the most per capita, and was 38th overall (immediately above Slovenia and one below Costa Rica).[20] It may well be that a connection exists between the extremely high costs of healthcare and the way in which physicians are compensated.

An optimal incentive approach for physicians may be the approach taken by the Mayo Clinic and the Cincinnati Clinic. They are considered two of the best healthcare facilities in the United States (and the world), and both pay their physicians a salary, rather than a piece rate system based on the number of patients seen and procedures or tests ordered.

5.5.2.4 *Wage Inequality*

There are a number of ways in which the new human science can help to eliminate wage inequality. The first is to accurately assess contribution through the use of advanced analytical techniques, including strategy maps, scorecards, and reward in line with actual contribution. Secondly, recognize that much potential value creation resides with those who are in direct contact with customers, the products and the innovation process, and providing an incentive to maximize that value is important. Furthermore, the information frontline employees possess is also valuable, and there should be an incentive to share or act on that information. Taking these steps should serve to both increase profits and disperse them more accurately to those who are responsible for making them.

Conclusion

The New Human Science is a combination of the new understanding of how we make decisions, our human nature, and developing technologies. These new combined insights and tools impact the way we make decisions, who we select, and how we select and motivate people.

In this book, I have shown how the new human science and advanced analytics can aid decision making; the critical role collaboration plays in organizational success; where value is derived from; and how eliminating biases from selection, promotion, and incentive decisions will also make for more equitable and successful workplaces. More information and tools to assist with decision making can be found at DecisionAnalyticsInc.com.

Much more needs to be done on this topic. More tools need to be built, and more topics need to be explored, including the following.

Garbage In...

This is so ubiquitous a problem that it hardly bears mentioning: All of this depends on the quality of the data. If we start with corrupted data, what we do with it and the insights it provides are largely useless.

Our Argumentative Natures

The English version of law, like much of academia, is largely based on an adversarial model. Both sides develop their argument as thoroughly as possible and fight tooth and nail. Obviously, there are upsides to this approach. However, the one tremendous downside is that neither side is really all that interested in the *truth* of what actually happened; they just want their side to win. This has the very unfortunate result of placing both sides in a position in which they deep six facts that might not support their specific position. The use of advanced analytics to better get at the facts of the matter needs much more attention.

Advanced Analytics and Diagnosis of HCM Issues

In 1999, then 3-year-old Isabel Maude came down with a high fever, vomiting, and a skin rash. The doctors diagnosed chicken pox but failed to identify the much more serious condition that developed: necrotizing fasciitis (or what is more commonly referred to as the flesh-eating disease). It took a substantial amount of time for the physicians to get the diagnosis right, and that delay almost cost Isabel her life. It also resulted in a long series of plastic surgery for Isabel.

The problem was anchoring bias. The doctors diagnosing the illness were simply certain that they had gotten it right. Had the flesh-eating disease occurred to them, they could have almost certainly made a more accurate diagnosis. One positive that came out of this near tragedy was Isabel's parents establishing the organization Isabel Health Care, which develops decision-support software for doctors. We need to develop an evidence-based deep Q&A expert system that can assist with determining human capital management (HCM) issues and solutions.

The Science (and Art) of Prediction

There are two ways to view the world: deterministically or probabilistically. It is difficult to argue that the world is entirely one or the other (although many hope we have some degree of free will). Though what we observe largely appears to be deterministic, we also see that the world seems to contain a healthy dose of randomness. The way products are arranged in a supermarket may not *cause* us to purchase goods, but it may increase the *likelihood*. We are not always going to choose the right employee, but if we apply some simple state-of-the-art decision mechanisms and techniques, we can increase the likelihood.

The Challenges with Being Empirically Declarative

These problems plague large-scale academic research because it is not clear whether we are really measuring employee engagement or effectiveness. It could well be something else that we have not identified that is actually causing the result we are seeing. Or it might be the proverbial cart-horse issue: Is the well-performing company pulling the engagement or effectiveness or vice versa? We can go some way toward reducing the impact of each of these problems, but it is difficult to eliminate them entirely.

One reason for many of the problems with these large-scale research projects is they would like to say something about generalizability. That is, do the effects observed apply to everyone? Each of these provides challenges to actually being able to declare unequivocally that the practices are causing the result. The unfortunate reality is that nearly all the academic research (including my own) suffers to some degree from one or more of these challenges. Fortunately, firms have a much better chance of conducting research into the impact of practice and policy choice for their specific situation, so generaliz-ability is less of an issue. Driving forward with information on "what works" is what is important, and the answer largely depends on when and where.

Decision-Making Authority and Cooperation

The critical issues that I want to develop in relationship to the Challenger story are these: where the critical information resides, who has the authority to make decisions, and the role of cooperation. The issue here is that there are many within the organization who have critical information, and they need to be in a position where they can share that information with decision makers.

Sharing Control and Return Rights

So, how do you foster an environment of collaboration? The answer is that you share control rights and return rights with your employees. There is powerful incentive effects associated with trans-ferring some of the rights of ownership to employees. Control rights are by definition the right of ownership that allows us to decide what we want to do with assets we own. Return rights are the rights to any revenue generated by those assets.

Individualization

Another potential benefit of advanced analytics is the ability to utilize technologies to tailor to the characteristics of the specific situation and the specific individual. There has long been a debate between the use of best practice and strategic choice. In essence, best practice research holds that there is a universal set of practices that everyone would benefit from using. Strategic choice holds that the situation dictates the specific policy and practice. I am firmly in the latter camp.

Have a look at the regression output using simple ordinary leased squared (OLS, a process of finding the line of best fit between data points by finding the difference between data points, allowing an estimate when the data is not available). Does anything strike you about the output? If you look closely at the line of best fit (the line running through the data points) either no one or very few actually fall directly on the line.

As we sequence our DNA, we can better individualize our healthcare and our nutrition. Similarly, advanced analytics will better allow us to get the right person in the right job and to determine what actually motivates that person as an individual.

Additional topics that need considerable thought include the following:

- **Agent-based modeling:** This could allow for a much more realistic model of how people actually respond to incentives or other interventions.

- **Neuroeconomics:** This emerging science has tremendous scope for better understanding decision making and how to do so more efficiently.

- **Combinatorics:** The branch of mathematics that provides insight into how rational decisions are made.

A

Definitions

This appendix provides fairly straightforward and easy-to-understand definitions. Most of these definitions have been sourced from Wikipedia, which I believe to be the premiere source for definitions. The alternative is to draw from a textbook on the subject (usually written by one to five authors). The crowdsourcing capacity of Wikipedia expands the number of experts providing input to dozens, hundreds, or even thousands, thus reducing the likelihood of bias and increasing the likelihood of including pertinent information.

Advanced analytics: According to Garter, Inc., advance analytics is defined[1] "as analysis of structured and unstructured content (such as text, images, video, voice) data using sophisticated quantitative methods (such as statistics, descriptive and predictive data mining, simulation, and optimization) to produce insights that traditional approaches to BI such as query and reporting are unlikely to discover. It is frequently applied to make decisions, solve business problems and identify opportunities by providing better forecasts, causal understanding, pattern identification, process and resource optimization, and assisting with scenario planning process."

Agent-based models: "Agent-based modeling (ABM) is a style of computational modeling that focuses on modeling individuals, components of individuals, or heterogeneous parts of a complex system. ABM as a style of computational modeling requires both mathematical and experimental approaches for its development and application."[2]

Artificial intelligence: Artificial intelligence (AI) is defined in various ways[3] in Russell and Norvig's book *Artificial Intelligence: A Modern Approach.* Essentially, AI is focused on *thought processes* and *reasoning.* Russell and Norvig further differentiate between how humans *actually* think and act and thinking and acting in an ideal manner (*rationally*). AI deals with both *actual* and *ideal* thinking and doing and how machines can mimic and assist this.[4]

Bayesian probability: Bayesian probability theory deals with uncertainty and decision making. This attempts to determine the probability of an event (A) occurring given that (B) has occurred. For example, you can determine the likelihood of employees leaving the organization (employee turnover) using Bayesian probability.[5]

Data mining: The essential definition of data mining is knowledge discovery in databases, which often follows these five steps:[6]

1. Selection
2. Pre-processing
3. Transformation
4. Data mining
5. Interpretation/evaluation

The emphasis of data mining is on discovering something new in the data.[7]

Decision trees: Decision trees are used to predict an item's likelihood based on observations of the item. Classification trees consist of determination of the likelihood of the occurrence of a class to which the data belongs. Regression trees are associated with the likelihood of a specific value (for example, price of house, hospital stay).[8]

Expert systems: Expert systems are computer programs that emulate the decision-making process. As the name implies, expert systems imitate the decision-making process of an expert. They contain a knowledge base and an inference engine. The knowledge base is the rules or "knowledge" created by the expert, and the inference engine is the reasoning used to derive recommendations from the knowledge base.[9]

Fuzzy logic: Fuzzy logic allows for nondichotomous answers that are found between 0 and 1 and are not a strict absolutely correct or absolutely false. This allows for reasoning that is approximate rather than precise. It can also be used to mimic nonrational outcomes (*fuzzjectives*).[10]

Genetic algorithms: A genetic algorithm is a search technique that borrows from processes found in evolution to find optimal solutions.[11]

Machine learning: "At its simplest, machine learning algorithms take an existing dataset, comb through it for patterns, and then use these patterns to generate predictions about the future."[12]

Neural nets: This term refers to the network of biological neurons. In the context of AI, neural nets are the artificial nodes used for developing predictive models.[13]

Endnotes

Introduction

1. IBM Global Business Services. (2010). "Working Beyond Borders."

2. An example is a recent *Wall Street Journal* article on how big data is being used to assist with hiring decisions. http://online.wsj.com/article/SB10000872396390443890304578006252019616768.html?mod=WSJ_hpp_MIDDLENexttoWhatsNewsThird.

3. http://www.marketplace.org/topics/business/added-value-autistic-employees.

4. Arrow, K. (1980). "Discrimination in the Labour Market," in J. E. King (ed.): *Readings in Labour Economics.* Oxford: Oxford University Press. Stigler, George. (1981). "Economics or ethics?" in S. McMurrin (ed.), *Tanner Lectures on Human Values,* Cambridge: Cambridge University Press. Williamson, Oliver. (1985). *The Economic Institutions of Capitalism.* New York: Free Press.

5. By far, the best way to overview the work of Fehr and others on these and other related topics is to go to Social Science Research Network. You can find much of his work there: http://papers.ssrn.com/sol3/results.cfm.

6. Kasparov, G. 2010 (February 11). "The Chess Master and the Computer," *New York Review of Books.*

Chapter 1

1. Thaler, R. and Sunstein, C. (2008). *Nudge: Improving Decisions About Health, Wealth and Happiness.* London: Penguin Books.

2. Others books that arrive at much the same conclusions include Richard Thaler and Cass Sunstein's book *Nudge*, 2009, London: Penguin Books; Robyn Dawes's *Everyday Irrationality*, 2001, Oxford: Westview Press; and Dan Ariely's *Predictably Irrational*, 2008, New York: HarperCollins.

3. Tversky, A. and Kahneman, D. (1981). "The Framing of Decisions and the Psychology of Choice," *Science, 211*, 453–458.

4. I would argue that the fight regarding whether effective human capital management impacts performance has been long won. See the work of Jac-Fitz Enz, Brian Becker, Mark Huselid, Casey Ichniowski, Ann Bartel, Katherine Shaw, and many others.

5. An excellent overview of the arguments is found in a book review by Philip Tetlock and Barbara Mellers in the January 2002 issue of the *Psychological Science Journal 13*(1), 94–99. The review is of the book *Choice, Values and Frames*, edited by Daniel Kahneman and Amos Tversky.

6. Kahneman, D. (2011). *Thinking, Fast and Slow.* New York: Farrar, Straus and Giroux. 212. The entire book deals with factors that influence our tendency to act rationally.

7. If you are interested, you can find much of this work at Social Science Research Network's ssrn.com, which is an excellent source of research.

8. Principal-agent theory states that there are owners and non-owners in firms. The owners incur costs in the form of incentive contracts to align the interests of the two parties. The incentive contracts themselves consist of a combination of formal monitors, substitutes for monitors, and direct incentives. Two issues that quickly surface with broad-based stock options are the free-rider and the line-of-sight problems. The free-rider problem argues that those receiving group incentives such as stock options will always be subject to "free riding" on the effort of others. The second is the line-of-sight problem, which is if your effort does not have a direct and obvious impact on the reward, there will be little incentive to focus on it. These two factors would suggest granting stock options to nonexecutives will have no material impact on performance.

9. In all of our research, we found a positive impact on performance associated with the granting of stock options broadly. However, in one of our last papers (July 2011, Sesil and Peng-Lin, *Industrial Relations*), we found that the impact of broad-based stock options was short-lived.

10. You can find a large amount of research on ownership culture and a variety of other research on employee ownership at the National Center for Employee Ownership. http://www.nceo.org/.

11. An interview with Thomas H. Davenport. July 2010, "Are You Ready to Reengineer Your Decision Making?."

12. Kahneman, D. (2011). *Thinking, Fast and Slow.* New York: Farrar, Straus and Giroux. 21.

13. Ibid. 22.

14. Blasi, J., Kruse, D., and Bernstein, A. (2003). *In the Company of Owners: The Truth About Stock Options.* New York: Basic Books.

15. Ibid.

16. Ibid. 5.

17. http://www.nytimes.com/2007/12/09/magazine/09wwln-idealab-t.html?_r=0.

18. You can find a more detailed explanation of each of these in Daniel Kahneman's *Thinking, Fast and Slow.* (2011). New York: Farrar, Straus and Giroux.

19. Thaler, R. H. and Sunstein, C. R. (2009.) *Nudge: Improving Decisions About Health, Wealth and Happiness.* New York: Penguin Books. 7.

20. Schoemaker, P. and Russo, J. "Managing Frames to Make Better Decisions," in Hoch, S. J., Kunreuther, H. C., and Gunther, R. E. (eds.). (2001). *Wharton on Making Decisions.* Hoboken, NJ: John Wiley & Sons, Inc. 131–155.

21. Ibid. 132–133.

22. http://en.wikipedia.org/wiki/Template:Quantities_of_bytes.

23. Zikopouloa, C., Eaton, C., deRoos, D., Deutsch, T., and Lapis, G. (2012). *Understanding Big Data: Analytics for Enterprise Class Hadoop and Streaming Data.* New York: McGraw Hill.

24. Rayer, N. (October 7, 2011). "Maverick Research: Judgment Day, or Why We Should Let Machines Automate Decision Making." Gartner Research Note. Gartner, Inc.

25. "Connecting the Neural Dots," (Tuesday, February 26, 2013), *New York Times,* Science Times section.

26. The articles can be found in the April 2011 issue of *Behavioral and Brain Sciences, 34,* 57–111.

27. Tetlock, P. (2005). *Expert Political Judgment: How Good Is It?* Princeton, NJ: Princeton University Press.

28. Klein, G. (2009). *Streetlights and Shadows: Searching for the Keys to Adaptive Decision Making.* Cambridge, MA: MIT Press. 125.

29. Hoch, S. J. and Kunreuther, H. C. (2001). "A Complex Web of Decisions," in Hoch, S. J., Kunreuther, H. C., and Gunther, R. E. (eds.). (2001). *Wharton on Making Decisions.* Hoboken, NJ: John Wiley & Sons, Inc.

30. Sallam, R. L. and Cearley, D. W. (February 16, 2012). "Advanced Analytics: Predictive, Collaborative and Pervasive." Gartner Research Note. Gartner Inc.

31. Ibid.

32. There is excellent work on this topic by, for example, Jac Fitz-Enz, *The New HR Analytics and The ROI of Human Capital.* Also by John Boudreau, *Retooling HR* and (with Peter Ramstad) *Beyond HR.*

33. Sallam, R. L. and Cearley, D. W. (February 16, 2012). "Advanced Analytics: Predictive, Collaborative and Pervasive." Gartner Research Note. Gartner Inc.

34. IBM Global Business Services. (2010). "Working Beyond Borders." The survey is based on interviews with 700 chief human resource managers.

35. Ibid. 2.

36. Ibid.

37. The formula was developed by John Tierney, the *New York Times* journalist and author, and Garth Sundem, self-proclaimed math geek and author. The formula was found in John Tierney's March 13 *New York Times* article "Refining the Formula That Predicts Celebrity Marriages' Doom," in the Science Times section.

38. Dawes, R. M. (1979). The robust beauty of improper linear models in decision making. *American Psychologist, 34*(7), 571–582.

39. Ayres, I. (2007). *Super Crunchers: Why Thinking-by-Numbers Is the New Way to Be Smart.* New York: Random House.

40. Power, D. J. (2002). *Decision Support Systems: Concepts and Resources for Managers.* Westport, CT and London: Quorum Books. 157.

41. Kahneman, D. (2011). *Thinking, Fast and Slow.* New York: Farrar, Straus and Giroux. 227.

42. Hoch, S. J. (2001). "Combining Models with Intuition," in Hoch, S. J., Kunreuther, H. C., and Gunther, R. E. (eds.). (2001). *Wharton on Making Decisions.* Hoboken, NJ: John Wiley & Sons, Inc.

43. Ibid. 100–101.

44. Yaser S. Abu-Mostafa. (July 2012). "Machines That Think for Themselves: New Techniques for Teaching Computers How to Learn Are Beating the Experts," *Scientific American,* 78.

45. Ibid.

46. Rayer, N. (October 7, 2011). "Maverick Research: Judgment Day, or Why We Should Let Machines Automate Decision Making." Gartner Research Note. Gartner, Inc.

47. Kasparov, G. (February 11, 2010). "The Chess Master and the Computer," *New York Review of Books.*

48. Iervilino, C. (February 17, 2012). "How to Leverage Advanced Analytics for Strategy Maps." Gartner Research, Gartner, 2012.

Chapter 2

1. Roger Boisjoly, an engineer at Morton Thiokol, the subcontractor responsible for manufacturing the O-rings, attempted repeatedly to have the launch stopped. However, his warnings were ignored. He spent much of this time after leaving Morton Thiokol lecturing widely on ethical fact-based decision making. http://www.onlineethics.org/CMS/profpractice/exempindex/RB-intro.aspx.

2. Berkes, H. (February 6, 2012). Remembering Roger Boisjoly: He Tried to Stop Shuttle Challenger Launch. National Public Radio Two Way Blog, Obituaries.

3. Ibid.

4. Davenport, T. H. (May 2012). "The Wisdom of Your In-House Crowd," *Harvard Business Review.*

5. Nowak, M. A. (December 8, 2006). "Five Rules for the Evolution of Cooperation," *Science, 314.* 1563.

6. Arrow, Kenneth. (1980). "Discrimination in the Labour Market," in J. E. King (ed.): *Readings in Labour Economics.* Oxford: Oxford University Press. Stigler, George. (1981). "Economics or ethics?" in S. McMurrin (ed.), *Tanner Lectures on Human Values,* Cambridge: Cambridge University Press. Williamson, Oliver. (1985). *The Economic Institutions of Capitalism.* New York: Free Press.

7. By far, the best way to overview the work of Fehr and others on these and other related topics is to go to Social Science Research Network. You can find much of his work there. http://papers.ssrn.com/sol3/results.cfm.

8. http://papers.ssrn.com/sol3/papers.cfm?abstract_id=717081.

9. http://papers.ssrn.com/sol3/papers.cfm?abstract_id=1090311.

10. The movie came out in 2001 and stared Russell Crowe and Jennifer Donnelly and was directed by Ron Howard. The movie is based on the book by the same name written by Sylvia Nasar and published in 1998.

11. E. O. Wilson, the Harvard evolutionary biologist who received the Pulitzer Prize for nonfiction for his book and is considered to be the founder of sociobiology.

12. Hopkins, M. (March 2010). "An Interview with Thomas W. Malone: A Billion Brains Are Better Than One," *MIT Sloan Management Review.*

13. Dean, L., Kendal, R., Schapiro, S., Thierry, B., and Laland, K. (March 2, 2012). "Identification of the Social and Cognitive Processes Underlying Human Cumulative Culture," *Science.*

14. Rozwell, C. (May 1, 2009). "Socialization of Knowledge Management Drives Greater Reuse." Gartner Research Note. Gartner, Inc.

15. Logan, D. (May 8, 2009). "Content Management Plus Organization Equals Knowledge Management." Gartner Research, Gartner Inc.

16. Shafei, F., Sundaram, D., and Piramuthu, S. (2012). "Multi-enterprise collaborative decision support system," *Expert System with Application, 39,* 7637–7651. This article has a focus more generally on the use of collaborative software in order to obtain information from external sources such as from customers and clients.

17. Thaler, R. and Sunstein, C. (2008). *Nudge: Improving Decisions About Health, Wealth and Happiness.* London: Penguin Books. In their books, they advance the notion of *libertarian paternalism,* which consists of the government steering us in the direction of better choices but in a manner that preserves freedom of choice.

18. Abele, J. (July-August 2011). "Bringing Minds Together," *Harvard Business Review.*

19. https://workfamily.sas.upenn.edu/sites/workfamily.sas.upenn.edu/files/imported/pdfs/SASwharton.pdf.

20. Davenport, T. H. (May 2012). "The Wisdom of Your In-House Crowd," *Harvard Business Review.*

21. Abele, J. (July-August 2011). "Bringing Minds Together," *Harvard Business Review.*

22. Ibid. 89.

23. Gilbert, M., Shegda, K., Chin, K., and Gavin, T. (October 13, 2011). "Magic Quadrant for Enterprise Content Management." Gartner Research, Gartner, Inc.

24. Ibid.

25. Sallam, R. (September 1, 2011). "Who's Who in Collaborative Decision Making." Gartner Research Note. Gartner, Inc.

26. Ibid.

Chapter 3

1. Kaplan, R. S. and Norton, D. P. (2004). *Strategy Maps: Converting Intangible Assets into Tangible Outcomes.* Boston: Harvard Business School Publishing.

2. http://www.businessweek.com/articles/2013-05-06/employers-love-wellness-programs-dot-but-do-they-work#r=hp-lst.

3. Lev's 2001 book *Intangibles Management, Measurement, and Reporting* (Washington D.C.: Brookings Institution Press) is an excellent overview of the role of intangibles and how to measure. An additional work is *Unseen Wealth: Report of the Brookings Task Force on Intangibles,* by Margaret M. Blair and Steven M. H. Wallman (Washington D.C.: Brookings Institution Press, 2001).

4. Ibid.

5. You can find a good discussion and overview of organizational capital in Lev and Radhakrishnana's (2003) "The Measurement of Firm-Specific Organizational Capital." NBER Working Paper # 9581.

6. Evenson, R. E. and Westphal, L. E. (1995). "Technological Change and Technological Strategy," in Behrman, J. and Srinivasan, T. N. (eds.), *Handbook of Development Economics 3e.* Amsterdam: North Holland, 2209–29.

7. Jovanovic, B. (1979). "Firm-Specific Capital and Turnover," *The Journal of Political Economy, 87*(6), 1246–60.

8. Rosen, S. (1972). "Learning by Experience as Joint Production," *The Quarterly Journal of Economics, 86*(3), 366–82.

9. Lin, Y. P. and Sesil, J. C. (July 2011). *British Journal of Industrial Relations, 49*(52), s402–s416.

10. Noe, R. A., Hollenbeck, J. R., Gerhart, B., and Wright, P. M. (2010). *Human Resource Management: Gaining a Competitive Advantage 7e.* New York: McGraw-Hill Irwin. 75.

11. Kaufman, B. K. and Miller, B. I. (April 2011). "The Firm's Choice of HRM Practice: Economics meets strategic human resource management," *Industrial and Labor Relations Review, 64,* 528.

12. Ibid.

13. Ibid. 526.

14. Ibid.

15. Anderson, D. R., Sweeney, D. J., Williams, T. A., Camm, J. D., and Martin, K. (2012). *An Introduction to Management Science: Quantitative Approaches to Decision Making.* Mason, OH: South-Western Cenage Learning.

16. The terms *management science* and *operation research* are currently considered interchangeable with *decision science* according to Anderson et.al., 2012.

17. Iervolino, C. (February 17, 2012). "How to Leverage Advanced Analytics for Strategy Maps." Research Note. Gartner, Inc.

18. This information was largely found in the IBM's Solution Brief "Business Analytics and Optimization–CFO performance dashboard–Advanced Edition," December, 2011. http://www-01. ibm.com/common/ssi/cgi-bin/ssialias?infotype=PM&infosubt= SP&htmlfid=gbs03077usen&appname.

19. In particular, the work of Casey Ichniowski, Kathryn Shaw, and Ann Bartel provides strong evidence of the impact of effective human capital management on organizational success.

20. Iervolino, C. (February 17, 2012). "How to Leverage Advanced Analytics for Strategy Maps." Gartner Research Notes, Gartner, Inc.

21. Evelson B. and Schooley, C. (November 7, 2011). "Use of HR Analytics to Optimize Talent Processes." Forrester Research Inc. Cambridge, MA.

22. Holincheck, J., Otter, T., and Freyermth, J. (February 29, 2012). Agenda for ERP and Enterprise Suites for Human Capital Management 2012.

23. There is sophisticated statistical analysis software used to analyze time series data. For example, STATA.

24. See SAS Talent Scorecard. http://www.sas.com/solutions/hci/hcscorecard/index.html#section=1.

25. Much good work on intangible capital has been done by Baruch Lev and can be found in his 2001 book *Intangibles Management, Measurement, and Reporting* (Washington D.C.: Brookings Institution Press).

26. Kaplan, R. S. and Norton, D. P. (2004). *Strategy Maps: Converting Intangible Assets into Tangible Outcomes.* Boston: Harvard Business School Publishing.

27. Holincheck, J. (May 10, 2011). "The Talent Management Suite Market Emerges." Gartner Research Note, Gartner, Inc.

28. Holincheck, J. (May 10, 2011). "The Talent Management Suite Market Emerges." Gartner Research Note, Gartner, Inc.

Chapter 4

1. Slaughter, A. M. (March 10, 2013). "Yes You Can," *New York Times Book Review*. This reviews the book by Sheryl Sandberg with Nell Scovell, *Lean In: Women, Work, and the Will to Lead*.

2. http://www.oecd.org/employment/emp/40937574.pdf.

3. http://www.npr.org/blogs/health/2013/04/22/177452578/young-adults-with-autism-can-thrive-in-high-tech-jobs.

4. This article in the *New York Times* is an excellent source of information on the use of big data and sophisticated analytics to assist with selection decisions. http://www.nytimes.com/2013/04/28/technology/how-big-data-is-playing-recruiter-for-specialized-workers.html?smid=fb-nytimes&WT.z_sma=TE_HBD_20130429&_r=0.

5. Ibid.

6. http://www.nytimes.com/2013/04/21/technology/big-data-trying-to-build-better-workers.html?pagewanted=all&_r=0.

7. http://www.foxbusiness.com/news/2013/03/12/rpt-yahoo-mayer-gets-internal-flak-for-more-rigorous-hiring/.

8. Ibid.

9. Bureau of National Affairs. (February 2011). "Pretty Women May Face Hiring Disadvantages, Study Finds," *H.R. focus* 88(2), 13.

10. "An Executive Perspective on Workforce Planning 2004." The Rand Corporation. Santa Monica, CA.

11. Kahneman, D. 2011. *Thinking, Fast and Slow*. New York: Farrar, Straus and Giroux. 246.

12. Ibid. 247.

13. Flyvbjerg, B. (January 2008). "Curbing Optimism Bias and Strategic Misrepresentation in Planning: Reference class forecasting in practice," *European Planning Studies, 16*(1), No. 1, 3–21.

14. Ibid. 8.

15. Glassdoor. http://www.crunchbase.com/company/glassdoor.

16. Garber, M. (March 20, 2012). "Would You Give Job Interviewers Your Facebook Password? Because They Might Ask." *The Atlantic.* http://www.theatlantic.com/technology/archive/2012/03/would-you-give-job-interviewers-your-facebook-password-because-they-might-ask/254810/.

17. Ibid. In Maryland, House Bill 364 was introduced in January 2012; and in Illinois, Illinois Bill 3782 was introduced in March 2012.

18. Hansell, S. (January 3, 2007). "Google's Answer to Filling Jobs Is an Algorithm," *New York Times.*

19. Dizikes, P. 2012. March 6th. "Hail to the geeks" MIT News Office.

20. Ibid.

21. Scarborough, D. J. et al. Electronic Employee Selection Systems and Methods. U.S. Patent No. 7,080,057 B2, filed August 2, 2001, and issued July 18, 2006. http://www.google.com/patents.

22. Breaugh, J. A. (2009). "The Use of Biodata for Employee Selection: Past research and future direction," *Human Resource Management Review, 19,* 219–231.

23. Ibid.

24. Goldsmith, D. B. (1922). "The Use of the Personal History Blank as a Salesmanship Test," *Journal of Applied Psychology, 6*(2), 149–155.

25. Ployhart, R. E., Schneider, B., and Schmitt, N. (2006). *Staffing Organizations: Contemporary Practice and Theory 3e.* Mahwah, NJ: Lawrence Erlbaum Associates.

26. Furnham, A. (2008). "HR Professionals' Beliefs About, and Knowledge of, Assessment Techniques and Psychometric Tests International," *Journal of Selection and Assessment, 16,* 300–305.

27. Ibid.

Chapter 5

1. http://www.ted.com/talks/dan_ariely_what_makes_us_feel_good_about_our_work.html.

2. http://www.gsb.stanford.edu/news/research/berk-incentives.html.

3. http://fcic-static.law.stanford.edu/cdn_media/fcic-testimony/2009-1020-Stiglitz-article.pdf.

4. http://papers.ssrn.com/sol3/papers.cfm?abstract_id=761970.

5. Bebchuk, L. and Fried, J. (2004). *Pay Without Performance: The Unfulfilled Promise of Executive Compensation*. Harvard University Press.

6. http://www.oecd.org/employment/emp/40846335.pdf.

7. Stigliz, J. E. (2012). *The Price of Inequality: How Today's Divided Society Endangers Our Future*. W.W. Norton & Company.

8. This may sound extreme, however, there were those who argued that the financial crisis was precipitated by excess risk taking, which was directly related to the way in which bankers and mortgage brokers were incented.

9. This YouTube video provides a good overview of the concept of marginal revenue product. http://www.youtube.com/watch?v=jhgTxU1q48g.

10. http://www.packers.com/community/shareholders.html.

11. Murphy, Audie (2002). *To Hell and Back*. New York: Henry Holt and Co.

12. Akerlof, G. A. (1982). "Labor Contracts as Partial Gift Exchange," *Quarterly Journal of Economics, 97,* 543–569.

13. Noe, R. A., Hollenbeck, J. R., Gerhart, B., and Wright, P. M. (2010). *Human Resource Management: Gaining a Competitive Advantage 7e.* New York: McGraw-Hill Irwin. 351.

14. Ibid. 354.

15. Harter, J. K., Schmidt, F. L., and Hayes, T. L. (2002). "Business-Unit Level Relationships between Employee Satisfaction, Employee Engagement, and Business Outcomes: A Meta-Analysis," *Journal of Applied Psychology, 87,* 88–95.

16. Latham, G., Almost, J., Mann, S., and Moore, C. (2005). "New Developments in Performance Management," *Organizational Dynamics, 34,* 77–87.

17. Evelson, G. and Schooley, C. (November 7, 2011). "Use of HR Analytics to Optimize Talent Processes." Forrester Research Inc. Cambridge, MA. Holincheck, J. (May 10, 2011). "The Talent Management Suite Market Emerges." Gartner Research Note. Gartner, Inc.

18. http://www.santafe.edu

19. Bebchuk, L. and Fried, J. (2004). *Pay Without Performance: The Unfulfilled Promise of Executive Compensation*. Harvard University Press.

20. http://en.wikipedia.org/wiki/World_Health_Organization_ranking_of_health_systems.

Appendix A

1. Sallam, R. L. and Cearley, D. W. (February 16, 2012). "Advanced Analytics: Predictive, Collaborative and Pervasive." Gartner Research Note. Gartner Inc.

2. This site provides a good introduction to agent-based modeling (ABM). ABM provides a method for modeling *actual* individual behaviors. http://www.agent-based-models.com/blog/about.

3. For these definitions, I draw heavily from Stuart Russell and Peter Norvig's *Artificial Intelligence: A Modern Approach 3e* (Pearson Education, 2010). This is largely taken from the Introduction, pages 1–5.

4. Ibid.

5. Giarratano, J. C. and Riley, G. D. (2005). *Expert Systems: Principles and Programming.* Boston: Thompson Learning, Inc.

6. Fayyad, U., Piatetsky-Shapiro, G. and Smyth, P. (1996). "From Data Mining to Knowledge Discovery in Database."

7. http://en.wikipedia.org/wiki/Data_mining.

8. http://en.wikipedia.org/wiki/Decision_tree_learning.

9. https://en.wikipedia.org/wiki/Expert_system.

10. http://en.wikipedia.org/wiki/Fuzzy_logic.

11. http://en.wikipedia.org/wiki/Genetic_algorithm.

12. Yaser S. Abu-Mostafa. (July 2012). "Machines That Think for Themselves: New Techniques for Teaching Computers How to Learn Are Beating the Experts," *Scientific American,* 78.

13. http://en.wikipedia.org/wiki/Neural_network.

Index

A

ABM (agent-based modeling),
127, 129
advanced analytics
defined, 13
expertise, combining with, 20-21
hierarchy of analytics, 14-17
adversarial nature of humans, 124
agency theory, 3
cooperation, 33
agent-based modeling (ABM),
127, 129
Agpar, Dr. Virginia, 20
AI (artificial intelligence), 22-23, 130
expert systems, 51-53
software applications, 25
tools, 25-26
algorithms, 23
genetic algorithms, 131
analytical thinking versus
intuition, 4-5
anchoring, 7
appraisal politics, impact on
performance management, 112
approaches to HCM practices, 67-69
argumentative reasoning, 11-12
Ariely, Daniel, 2, 101
artificial intelligence (AI), 22-23, 130
expert systems, 51-53
software applications, 25
tools, 25,26
asymmetric information, 37-38, 83-84

B

Barton, Richard, 93
Bebchuk, Lucian, 119
Besse, Tim, 93
best practices, 65-67
BI (business intelligence)
advanced analytics, 13-14
collaborative BI, 50-51
and decision science, 70-72
biases
anchoring, 7
appraisal politics, 112
confirmation bias, 7
in empirical research, 61
framing, 7-8
impact on performance
management, 112-113
loss aversion, 7
removing from decision making,
xvii-xviii, 81-82
similar to me bias, 112
status quo, 7
big data, 9
bio data, as employee selection
tool, 93-98
BizX, optimal HCM practice
selection, 74-75
Bloomberg, Michael, 42
Boisjoly, Roger, 28
Boston Scientific, as model for
collaboration, 48
Buffet, Warren, 11

business intelligence (BI)
  advanced analytics, 13-14
  collaborative BI, 50-51
  and decision science, 70-72

C

CDM (collaborative decision making) software, 51-53
CEP (Center for Economic Performance), 59
certitude, 10
challenges with forecasting, 90-92
collaboration, 34-35
  benefits of, 41-42
  Boston Scientific, 48
  EMC, 47-48
  incentive contracts for, 44-45
  participative decision making, 42-43, 49-50
  prisoners' dilemma, 38-39
  SAS Institute, 46-47
  the Scandinavian model, 39-43
  and tournament compensation, 107
collaborative BI, 50-51
collaborative decision making (CDM) software, 51-53
collecting human capital data, 59-61
collective intelligence, 36-37
collusion, 34
combinatorics, 127
combining expert intuition and analytics, 20-21
commoditizing human capital, 56
comparing analytical thinking and intuition, 4-5
compensation packages, 104-105, 107-108
  executive compensation, applying to human sciences, 118-120
  piece rates, 106
complexity theory, 115
configurational approach to HR practices, 67
confirmation bias, 7
contingency approach to HR practices, 67

control rights, 44-45
  sharing, 126
cooperation, 32-33
  asymmetric information, 37-38
  game theory, 32-35
  prisoners' dilemma, 38-39
  ratcheting, 35-36
  and reciprocity, 32-33
corporate culture, 43-44
critical information, importance of sharing, 126

D

data mining, 130
Davenport, Thomas, 4
Dawes, Robyn, 2
Dawes formula, 18
decision making
  AI, software applications, 25
  analytical thinking versus intuition, 4-5
  biases, 6
    anchoring, 7
    confirmation bias, 7
    framing, 7-8
    loss aversion, 7
    removing, xvii-xviii, 84
    status quo, 7
  certitude, 10
  critical information, importance of sharing, 126
  descriptive, 12
  and equity, xviii-xix
  expert systems, 51-53
  "framing effect," 2
  HCM decisions, xvii-xx
  human nature, 6
  intuition, xvi-xvii, 4-5
  normative, 12
  participative, 42-43, 49-50
  prescriptive, 12
decision science, 70-72
  BI, 70-72

decision trees, 130
   applying to incentive issues, 117
   employee selection, applying to, 99-100
DecisionAnalyticsInc.com, xx
deep Q&A expert systems, 99
descriptive decision making, 12
deterministic world view, 125
diagnosing problems with HCM, 124
dishonesty, 30-31

E

ECM (enterprise content management) software, 49
econometrics, applying to incentive issues, 117-118
economic impact of collaboration, 42-43
econs, 1-2
Edgar database, 119
efficiency wage, 108
eliminating bias, 81-82, 84
EMC, as model for collaboration, 47-48
empirical research
   bias in, 61
   generalizability, 126
employee selection
   biases, removing, 84-86
   human sciences, applying to
     AI, 99-100
     deep Q&A expert systems, 99
     expert intuition, 98
     game theory, 99
     machine learning, 99-100
     predictive modeling, 99
   incentives, 104-105
     compensation packages, 104-105
     piece rates, 106
   motivations of individuals, identifying, 103-107
     compensation packages, 104-105

with social analytics, 92-93
using bio data, 93-98
workforce planning, 87-88
   and predictive analytics, 88-89
enterprise content management (ECM) software, 49
enterprise resource planning (ERP) software
   optimal HCM practices, selecting, 75-76
equity in decision making, xviii-xix
ERP (enterprise resource planning) software
   optimal HCM practices, selecting, 75-76
evaluating performance, 112-113
executive compensation
   applying human sciences to, 118-120
   indexation, 120
experimental philosophy, 6
expert intuition, applying to incentive issues, 115-116
Expert Maker, 25
expert systems, 22, 130
   applying to incentive issues, 116-117
   for CDM, 51-53
   deep Q&A expert systems, 99
   Expert Maker, 25
expertise, combining with advanced analytics, 20-21

F

fairness, 29-30
Fehr, Ernst, 31
financial rewards to incentive contracts, 114-115
"The Firm's Choice of HRM Practices: Economics Meets Strategic Human Resource Managementy," 67
Flyvbjerg, Bent, 91
forecasting
   challenges with, 90-92
   inside view, 91
   outside view, 91
   reference class forecasting, 91-92